LANGUAGE AND STUDY SKILLS

FOR LEARNERS OF ENGLISH

Marjorie Reinwald Romanoff, Ed.D.
American Language Institute
University of Toledo
Toledo, Ohio

PRENTICE HALL REGENTS
Englewood Cliffs, New Jersey 07632

Library of Congress Cataloging-in-Publication Data

Romanoff, Marjorie R. (Marjorie Reinwald). (date)
  Language and study skills for learners of English / Marjorie R.
Romanoff.
     p.   cm.
  Includes bibliographical references.
  ISBN 0-13-847229-7
  1. Study, Method of.   2. Language arts (Higher)   3. Reading
(Higher education)   4. Examinations—Study guides.   I. Title.
LB2395.R745   1991
378.1'70281—dc20   90-21433
                                                          CIP

Editorial/production supervision
and interior design: **Shirley Hinkamp**
Acquisitions Editor: **Anne Riddick**
Development Editor: **Helen Munch**
Cover design: **Patricia Kelly**
Pre-Press buyer: **Ray Keating**
Manufacturing buyer: **Lori Bulwin**
Photo research: **Kay Dellosa**

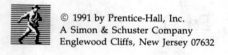 © 1991 by Prentice-Hall, Inc.
A Simon & Schuster Company
Englewood Cliffs, New Jersey 07632

Printed in the United States of America
10 9 8 7 6 5 4 3 2 1

ISBN 0-13-847229-7

Prentice-Hall International (UK) Limited, *London*
Prentice-Hall of Australia Pty. Limited, *Sydney*
Prentice-Hall Canada Inc., *Toronto*
Prentice-Hall Hispanoamericana, S.A., *Mexico*
Prentice-Hall of India Private Limited, *New Delhi*
Prentice-Hall of Japan, Inc., *Tokyo*
Simon & Schuster Asia Pte. Ltd., *Singapore*
Editora Prentice-Hall do Brasil, Ltda., *Rio de Janeiro*

Dedication

This book was written in loving memory of our dearest daughter, Janet Beth; in honor of my beloved husband, Milford, our children, Dr. Bennett and Hedva, Lawrence and Deborah, and our grandchildren, Daniel, David, Lauren Beth, Michelle, Jennifer Beth, Michael, and Steven Romanoff.

The author thanks the following for their cooperation and permission to use copyrighted material: Dr. Gloria Freimer, Research Librarian, and Denise Green, visiting librarian, The University of Toledo for the list of library terms on pp. 12–14; S. I. Hayakawa, *Language in Action: A Guide to Accurate Thinking, Reading, and Writing*, New York: Harcourt Brace and Co., 1942, for the information on p. 47; Joseph Gallo and Henry Rink, *Shaping College Writing: Paragraph and Essay* for the figure on p. 48. © 1985 by Harcourt Brace Jovanovich. Reprinted by permission of the publisher. Raymond S. Henry, The University of Toledo Community College, Communications Department for the list of transitions, p. 55; Judith Hanaken, PhD., The University of Toledo Community and Technical College, Communications Department, 1976, for "Nosy Nora," p. 56; R. Ornstein and R. F. Thompson, *The Amazing Brain*, Boston: Houghton Mifflin Co., 1984, for the information about the brain, p. 56, *Occupational Outlook Handbook*, U. S. Dept. of Labor, Bureau of Statistics, Bulletin 220, 17, U.S.C. #403, 1982–83 Edition, for "Administrative and Managerial Occupations" on p. 59; Thomas Blotter, *Introduction to Engineering*, copyright © 1981. Reprinted by permission of John Wiley & Sons, for "Engineering Challenges," p. 60; Francis P. Robinson, *Effective Reading*, New York: Harper & Row (1962) for the formula adapted on p. 75. © 1962 by Francis Robinson. Reprinted by permission of Harper Collins Publishers.

Keith Carter, *USA TODAY*, Sept. 5, 1990 "Highway Deaths Show Decline," for graphs G and H; Copyright 1990, *USA TODAY*. Reprinted with permission. Toledo—Lucas County Port Authority, Toledo, Ohio, for graph B; Michael D. Thorne, *USA TODAY*, June 22, 1990 "States With the Most Little League Teams," for graph D; Jeff Dionise, *USA TODAY*, July 16, 1990, "Men in the Marketplace" for graph E; Copyright 1990, *USA TODAY*. Reprinted with permission. American Language Institute, University of Toledo, 1990, for graph J; Keith Carter, *USA TODAY*, June 28, 1990, "The Federal Budget," for graph I; Copyright 1990, *USA TODAY*. Reprinted with permission; John Paxton, Ed. *Statesman's Yearbook*, 122nd. edition, New York: St. Martins Press, 1985–86; for table on p. 93. Reprinted by permission of St. Martins Press and Macmillan Press.

Lawrence J. Gitman and Carl McDaniel, Jr., *Business World*, New York: John Wiley & Sons, 1983, for the information on p. 94; *Encyclopedia Americana, Vol. 2*, 1978 for adaptation on "Atmosphere," p. 95; *World Book Encyclopedia* (1986), for adaptation on "Apes" by J. R. Napier on p. 99; Vernon A. Musselman and John H. Jackson, *Introduction to Modern Business*, Ninth Edition, Englewood Cliffs, New Jersey: Prentice-Hall, Inc., 1984, for the passages on p. 105; James M. Barrett; Peter Abramoff; A. Krishna Kumaran; William S. Millington; *Biology*, Englewood, Cliffs, N.J.: Prentice-Hall Inc., 1986, for adaptation on p. 109.

Acknowledgments

I would like to express my deepest thanks to the many people who have encouraged and facilitated the writing of my ideas down into book form.

First of all, I am indebted to Dr. Pamela Sharpe, who was the director of the American Language Institute at The University of Toledo for several years. She sought me out to work on curriculum and also to develop and teach a course called "Study Skills." After my first term there, she encouraged me to write a book on the subject and kept urging me until I relented six years later. Without her guidance, critical proofreading, and continuous support, this book would not have been written.

I am also grateful to Dr. Karen Miller of the Community and Technical College of the University of Toledo for her openness and intellectual generosity. Many of the ideas in Unit 2 of this book were formulated after I daily observed this remarkable young woman as she taught a course in communications. Her course was developed together with Dr. Judith Hanaken and Dr. Raymond S. Henry of the same college. Dr. Hanaken created the Nosy Nora paragraph (Unit 3) that has such universal appeal, and Dr. Henry created several outlines and word groupings. My course on study skills was developed around the ideas that these three special people created.

Dr. Gloria Freimer, a brilliant research librarian at The University of Toledo, responded enthusiastically to my request for a vocabulary list that would be necessary for students to adequately utilize library services. Her added suggestions, as well as her ability to do deep and critical listening, are deeply appreciated.

Without Lisa Romanoff of Prentice Hall, I might not have had the opportunity to publish with such an outstanding publisher. She kept after me to publish with them and introduced me to Brenda White, my original editor.

Anne Riddick subsequently became my editor, and her enthusiasm, as well as assurances, were more appreciated than she can know. She introduced me to Helen Munch, my development editor, who deleted extraneous material, designed the format, and gained my respect as a genius at organization. Her knowledge of ESL proved to be invaluable to me. My thanks, also, to Shirley Hinkamp for her insightful supervision.

Of all my reviewers, the most thorough reading and valuable feedback came from Dr. Cristin Carpenter. For her time, energy, and brilliant analysis I am forever grateful.

To Rollind Romanoff, my more than competent attorney, I express my thanks for his generous advice.

Barbara Monger has done typing for me for almost two decades and is much more than a typist. Her feedback and suggestions, as well as her diligence and positive attitude, proved to be indispensable in producing this book.

To the former dean of the Continuing Education Center at The University of Toledo, the late Dr. Thomas Clapp, I am very grateful for making a word processor available and for allowing us to use the facilities until very late hours. His enthusiasm for this endeavor was very encouraging. Also, to the administrators, teachers, and staff of the ALI, I thank each one for the kind words, extra typing, and general support that was given in such great measure. Linda Jackson, of the ALI, deserves special appreciation for field testing this material for several terms. In addition, I am indebted to Barbara Sayers for her expert proofreading. Their feedback was invaluable.

My parents, David E. and Gertrude Reinwald, who died while I was in the process of writing this book, looked forward to its production. I am eternally grateful to them for raising me with the kind of discipline that has given me a good self-concept and for instilling in me the idea that life is a constant search for the development of all of one's talents and abilities. Their unequivocal love and support has been selfless and exemplary. In addition, one of my most enthusiastic supporters was my mother–in–law, Edythe Romanoff Bort, who also died while I was in the process of producing the book. To her I am grateful for her faith in me, as well as her great love.

I have given credit to all kinds of people, but, without the desire to impart composition and study skills to our seven wonderful grandchildren, I am certain that I would not have organized these ideas and put them down on paper. To Daniel, David, Lauren Beth, Michelle, Jennifer Beth, Michael, and Steven, I can only say that our love for you is an inspiring force in our lives.

Last, to my talented, and indeed, remarkable husband, Milford M. Romanoff, there are no words to adequately express the good fortune I feel at being married to the most selfless person I have ever known. He has encouraged me to write a book for the past forty years; he has facilitated me through masters and doctors degrees; he has relieved me of all kinds of responsibilities in order to give me time to be productive. A creative artist himself, he has done an illustration and conceived the idea for the cover of this book.

Contents

To the Student

To do well in an American university, you need to learn certain skills and concepts. *Language and Study Skills for Learners of English* was written to help you learn these skills and concepts so that you can succeed in your academic life in the United States.

Using this book, you will learn how to establish good study habits, develop your vocabulary, organize your writing, improve your reading, and take university exams. You will read and review different examples and do related exercises, either in your book or on a separate piece of paper.

If you read the text, study the examples closely, and do the exercises carefully, you will meet with success in your work. However, if you fail to pay attention or are frequently absent from class, you may miss a lot.

Ask your instructor or a friend for help if you need it when you are using this textbook. There is a lot of information on these pages that can be useful to you. But you must make an effort to do your best.

Good luck!

Introduction

•About This Book

In recent years there has been a renewal of interest in study skills for students of English as a second or foreign language (ESL or EFL students). Courses have been developed either as adjuncts to content curriculum or as components of language skills programs.

Language and Study Skills for Learners of English was written to meet the needs of instructors and intermediate-to-advanced–level students in intensive English programs (IEPs) in the United States. It may also be of interest to ESL students in regular university-level English, speech, and communication courses and/or to ESL/EFL students in colleges and private programs abroad.

•How This Book Is Organized

Language and Study Skills for Learners of English is divided into six units, each one focusing on specific language and study skills and offering examples of and practice in each.

Each unit opens with a checklist of questions regarding particular information presented in that unit. Depending on how they answer the questions, students may skip portions of the unit and read the indicated pages and do the accompanying exercises in the book. The activities and exercises are designed to involve students as much as possible with their own specific language and study needs and materials.

Unit 1: Getting Started is an orientation unit to help students find their way around, adjust to campus life, and develop good study habits. Map and information-gathering exercises are included to help students become familiar and comfortable with their new academic surroundings.

Unit 2: Developing Your Vocabulary encourages students to become "word collectors" and to increase their English vocabulary by familiarizing themselves with an English-only dictionary, and by learning how words are formed using prefixes, stems, and suffixes. Practice in recognizing words in context is also a part of this unit.

Unit 3: Organizing Your Writing examines the skill of outlining as it is used *before* students begin to write. Topic and sentence outlines are introduced and practiced prior to the study of paragraphs (topic, supporting, and concluding sentences, and transitions) and essays (thesis statement, supporting paragraphs, and conclusion).

Unit 4: Improving Your Reading offers students the additional skills of previewing a textbook, skimming, scanning, outlining, and mapping a reading text, and making use of graphic aids. The unit ends with a brief treatment of summary writing, also.

Unit 5: Practicing Notemaking introduces the skill of making notes from printed as well as spoken texts. Students learn the importance of abbreviations and practice using them while making notes.

Unit 6: Taking Exams discusses the different examination types—objective and subjective—and offers advice for enhancing performance on true/false, multiple-choice, fill-in-the-blank, matching, and essay exams.

Each unit ends with extension activities related to the skills presented and practiced in that unit, followed by answers to the unit exercises.

•How to Use This Book

Language and Study Skills for Learners of English is designed for use as a textbook-workbook with the whole class and on an individual student basis. While the units may be presented in any order, it is recommended that all students begin by reviewing the orientation and study habits information presented in Unit 1. Thereafter, students may proceed at their own pace, either with the class or on their own, working with the chapter-opening checklists and reading the material indicated. By doing the exercises in the book, students have a chance to implement the skills they have been reading about and relating them to their own academic situations. While most of the exercises are intended to be done by students working alone, some exercises can be handled cooperatively by students working together in small groups (for example, using the library, using prefixes, stems, and suffixes, and making an outline). It is expected that the instructor will be circulating among students to answer questions and check progress.

The objective of *Language and Study Skills for Learners of English* is to empower students to perform effectively and with confidence in their new academic environment. To that end, students are urged to *try out* their new skills as often as possible, both while studying in an intensive English program and when enrolled in subject area courses at the college or university level. By continuing to practice the skills presented in this book, students will become better able to comprehend the academic world around them and, little by little, be able to participate in it.

If you have read and understood this Introduction, you are ready to start with Unit 1 of this book.

Unit 1
Getting Started

●Finding Your Way Around (Answer Yes or No)

●Establishing Good Study Habits

●Using the Library

If you answered "NO" to any of the questions above, read the indicated pages and do the corresponding exercises.

•Finding Your Way Around

Knowing your way around campus and how to find key offices and buildings is an important part of "settling in" at a university. Knowing where to go, whom to contact, and how to use your university student services can be a big help, too.

The Campus Tour

Most colleges and universities arrange campus tours for visitors and new students. These tours are lead by student campus guides and, sometimes, by staff or faculty. The tours generally last one-half hour to an hour and usually include visits to the administrative offices, individual departments or schools, the main university library, student health and financial services, the bookstore, the cafeteria, student sports areas, and student residences or dormitories. A tour is a good way to get to know your campus and to learn more about student life. It is also a good way for you to practice asking questions and listening for answers in English!

If you have already taken a tour of your campus, go on to *exercise 1*.

Exercise 1: Campus Tour

Draw or staple a map of your campus on this page. Identify the main areas of importance to you on your campus.

Student Services

In order to help students find housing and obtain financial aid, most universities offer special services. Information on where to look for off-campus housing—apartments or rooms to rent, or homes to share—is usually available from the student housing service. Applications and information about financial aid, such as scholarships, student loans, and work/study programs, can be found at most student financial aid offices.

Health services for enrolled students are generally available on campus or through a local hospital near campus. Students must typically purchase university-sponsored health insurance in order to participate in a health-care program and to receive medical service.

Other student services may be available on your campus. When inquiring about them, be sure to present your student identification (ID).

If you are familiar with your school's student services, go on to *exercise 2*.

Exercise 2: Student Services

Record the location and hours of operation of each of the following services.

	Location	Hours
1. Student housing office		
2. Financial aid office		
3. Health service		

Record below the name, identification number, and effective date of your student health insurance: _____

International Student Services/Student Advisor

Laima Druskis

In addition to the regular student services offered to all university students, some universities offer special academic, social, and counseling services to their international students. Use of such services may require a membership fee that is used to cover the cost of special sports activities, field trips, parties, special classes, holiday events, and music or cultural programs.

International students may also be assigned a counselor or a student advisor, who can be of assistance in coping with academic or adjustment problems.

If you have a student advisor, go on to *exercise 3*.

Exercise 3: Student Advisor

Write the name and telephone number of your advisor and when/where he or she can be reached.

Name:
Telephone number:
Office:
Hours

•Establishing Good Study Habits

Good study habits are crucial for your success in the university. Scheduling your time, having an appropriate place to study, and learning how to study alone or with other people are all habit forming. By establishing good study habits when you arrive at your university, you will ensure yourself a successful start in your academic life.

Scheduling Your Time

When registering for classes, consider the times of day you do your best work. Try to schedule your classes at those hours. Be sure to leave an hour or two free each day for exercise, chores (shopping, laundry, and so on), and relaxation with others.

Whether you are a "morning person" or an "afternoon person," you will want to leave enough time in your daily schedule to prepare and study for classes. And, if you share a room with another student, you'll need to consider your roommate's schedule and study habits as well as your own.

For help in planning your daily schedule, turn to *p. 6, exercise 4.*

Exercise 4: Schedule Planning

Fill in your daily schedule below. Include the days and hours of your classes and any other "scheduled" time you have.

	Sun.	Mon.	Tues.	Wed.	Thurs.	Fri.	Sat.
7:00–8:00AM							
8:00–9:00							
9:00–10:00							
10:00–11:00							
11:00–12:00							
12:00–1:00PM							
1:00–2:00							
2:00–3:00							
3:00–4:00							
5:00–6:00							
7:00–8:00							
8:00–9:00							
9:00–10:00							
10:00–11:00							
11:00–12:00							
12:00–1:00AM							

Choosing a Place for Study

Where you study is as important as *when* you study. There are many places where you might feel comfortable with a book. But these places might not be ideal when it comes to studying or preparing for classes.

Peter Menzel/Stock, Boston

A good place for study should have some, if not all, of these features: a separate desk or table used only for studying; a desk lamp or an overhead light that provides adequate lighting (100-watt bulbs are good for desk work); an English-only dictionary and other reference books you need for your classes; a hard-backed but comfortable chair that allows you to sit straight while you work.

If you share a room with another student, be sure it is clear where each of you plans to study, and when. Talking about your individual habits, preferences, and schedules ahead of time will help you to avoid conflicts later on.

Turn to *p. 8, exercise 5,* to evaluate your place of study.

Exercise 5: Place of Study

Look at the list below and check whether or not your place of study offers the indicated features.

	1. A separate desk or table
	2. A hard-backed chair
	3. A desk lamp or an overhead light (100-watt bulb or stronger)
	4. An all-English dictionary
	5. Other reference books for class
	6. Writing supplies (or a typewriter, computer)

Knowing How to Study

Having a good place and time for study can facilitate studying and the formation of good study habits. But knowing *how to use* your study time wisely is also essential. For example, when you are studying for a class, do you play your radio, television, or stereo? Does music, talking, or background noise disturb you? Do you smoke? Are you tempted to smoke, eat, or drink while you are studying? Do you have a telephone in your room? Do people phone you or do you make frequent telephone calls during your scheduled study period? Do friends stop by to visit you when you are studying?

Sometimes other habits, such as smoking or listening to the radio while studying, actually help one concentrate on a task. Other times these habits may be distractions. It's important for you to know what helps and what interferes with your own study habits and schedule. In that way you can better use and control your study time.

Studying with Others

While many students prefer to study alone, there may be times when studying with one or two of your classmates can be of mutual benefit. First of all, you will have an opportunity to improve your English by expressing your ideas in a small group. Secondly, you will have a chance to compare what you've heard, read, or learned in class with what your classmates know. And finally, you will get to know some of your classmates better and perhaps become friends.

Responding in Class

While many American instructors are informal in class and may ask that you address them by their first or given name, not all instructors feel the same. Unless your instructor requests you to use his or her first name, it is better to use *Mr.*, *Mrs.*, or *Ms.*, with the person's family name or surname. If your instructor has received a doctorate degree (PhD or EdD) or holds the rank of professor, use *Doctor* _____ or *Professor* _____. If you are unsure of your instructor's status, ask.

Laima Druskis

When responding in class, it is always wise to raise your hand before you speak to get the instructor or another student's attention. If you have a specific question to ask your instructor, one that might take up too much class time, it may be best to ask it after class has ended. Again, your instructor will be able to tell you what his or her expectations are regarding in-class behavior.

Doing Homework

While many instructors emphasize in-class participation and work done in class, most expect a fair amount of study to be done outside of class in the form of homework assignments. To do your best on out-of-class assignments, be sure, first of all, that you understand what each assignment requires. Are you to read one chapter only in a book? Should you prepare an outline or write a summary? Will the instructor be discussing the same chapter in the next class? Are you supposed to write a paper? Record each assignment on a separate page of your notebook or in a pocket calendar book so that **you know exactly what the assignment is and when it is due.** Most instructors expect assignments to be turned in on time and may deduct points if you hand a paper in late. Check to see what your instructor's policy is regarding work that is late.

Another point to remember when doing out-of-class assignments is to make sure that work that you do is your own. Many times when writing research reports involving the use of library books, students mistakenly copy material from the books into their own reports. Using someone else's work and giving them credit for it (or citing their name and publication in a footnote as a reference) is permissible. However, copying someone else's work and claiming it as your own is a serious academic offence known as *plagiarism*. Be sure that you acknowledge the source of any copyrighted work that you include in your own writing. If you are unsure of a particular source, tell your instructor or librarian. They may be able to direct you to a sourcebook for help.

•Using the Library

Hugh Rogers/Monkmeyer Press

One of a university's most valuable resources is its library. Before you finish your university studies, you will spend many hours in the library, either reading or searching for books, magazines, and other publications that will help you with your studies. A visit to the library is almost always included in a campus tour; however, many libraries offer their own separate tours to orient students to their particular services. Be sure you take a library tour to acquaint yourself with your library's hours of operation and way of doing things.

If you have visited your school library, turn to *p. 12, exercise 6.*

Exercise 6: Library Hours

Record below the hours that your school library is open.

Monday	
Tuesday	
Wednesday	
Thursday	
Friday	
Saturday	
Sunday	

How long may you keep a book from your school library? _____

Vocabulary of the Library

Many words used to refer to the library, its books, and its functions form part of a special library vocabulary that students need to know. Listed below are some common library terms along with their explanations. Become familiar with these terms, so that you can communicate effectively with library staff and make good use of the library's resources.

abbreviation – a short form of a word

abstract – a brief summary giving the important points of a book or article

alphabetical – listed in order of the letters of the alphabet

article – a piece of writing, usually nonfiction, that appears in a journal or magazine

author – a person who writes a book, article, or play

autobiography – the story of a person's life written by that person

biography – the story of a person's life written by another person

bibliography – a list of books, articles, documents, and other resources concerned with a particular topic or subject area

bound – held together by a strong material and a cover

call number – a set of numbers and letters that identify a particular book in a library

catalog – a list that records, describes, and indexes the collection in a library

computer searching – using a computer to locate information in a data base

copyright date – the year in which a book or article was first published

current issues – the most recent copies of a magazine or journal

encyclopedia – a reference work containing an overview of informational articles on a wide variety of subjects

entry – a record of a book in a catalog or list

illustration – any chart, map, table, graph, picture, or photo that appears in a publication

index (in a book) – a list of items, arranged in alphabetical and numerical order, that assists you in locating topics in a book

index (subject matter) – a guide that enables you to find books and articles in a library or resource center

issue – a single, dated, numbered part of a magazine, journal, or newspaper

microform, microfiche, microfilm – the reproduction in reduced form—on paper, a card, or film—of library material

periodical – a publication, such as a magazine or journal, that appears at regular intervals (weekly, monthly) and contains articles by several authors

photocopy – the process of copying a text by photographing it by machine

publisher – the company responsible for releasing a piece of writing in printed form

research – a systematic, exhaustive, and intensive investigation of a subject in order to discover new knowledge, facts, theories, and laws

search strategy – a systematic method of looking for information

subheading – that part of a description of a topic that lies beneath the description and further narrows the topic

subject (heading) – the primary theme or topic on which a work is focused

table of contents (or Contents) – a list of articles in a periodical or a list of units/chapters in a book, found at the front of each periodical or book

title – the name of any written work

topic – the subject of a written work

volume – a book or series of issues of a periodical, bound together

If you studied the library vocabulary carefully, go on to *exercise 7*.

Exercise 7: Library Vocabulary

Using the vocabulary listed, identify the information on the library catalog card on p. 15. (Refer to the explanations on pages 12–14 if you need help.)

author _____ **call number** _____

title _____

copyright date

publisher _____ _____

number of pages _____ **subject heading** _____

illustrations? yes: _____ **no:** _____

```
616        Meilach, Dona Z.
.73          How to relieve your aching back /
           Dona Z. Meilach ; foreword by John R.
           Lake ; photographs by Dona and Mel
           Meilach. -- New York : Bantam, c1979.
             41 p. : ill. ; 20 cm.

             Bibliography: p. 40-41.
             ISBN 0-553-01216-9


             1. Backache.  2. Exercise therapy.
           I. Title.
ALCO           810417       CHA
L000713        PG /VIC      A*        23230959
```

Compare your answers with those on p. 18.

Finding a Book

Before the age of computers, card catalogs served as the inventory of a library's holdings. Books were listed on individual cards that were filed alphabetically by title, author, and subject heading. Nowadays, computers have replaced most card catalogs, but the method of "cataloging" books remains much the same.

In order to find out if your library has a book that you want, "call up" the book on the computer, giving the title, author, or subject heading of the book. Or, if your library lacks a computer, consult the card catalog. If the book is part of your library's collection, a special number referred to as a *call number* will appear. Once you know the book's call number you can either look for the book yourself on the shelves—if your library has "open stacks" and allows you to do this—or you can ask a librarian to assist you.

Now turn to *p. 16, exercise 8* for help in finding a book.

Exercise 8: Finding a Book

Using your library's card catalog or computer, look up the title, author, or subject heading of a book that you want. Record the information you find below.

Subject:
Title:
Author:
Call number:
Other information:

Using References and Periodicals

Besides thousands of books, a library has many references and periodicals for people to borrow and use. References such as dictionaries, atlases, encyclopedias, yearbooks, special indexes, and bibliographies are usually listed in the card catalog with the notation *REF.* to indicate reference material. References are generally shelved separately in a library's reference room and they are not allowed to be borrowed or to circulate. Periodicals such as magazines, journals, and newspapers that are published at particular times — daily, weekly, monthly, annually — are listed in the ***Reader's Guide to Periodical Literature*** and can be found in the reference room or in another part of the library. Some libraries allow periodicals to be checked out for a short time. Be sure to ask your librarian about your school's check-out policy and for help in using the ***Reader's Guide.***

For practice using references and periodicals, go on to *exercise 9.*

Exercise 9: Using References and Periodicals

Ask your librarian if you need help in completing this exercise.

1. Find a reference book that contains information about your country. Record the requested information below:

   Title of book: _____

   Copyright date: _____

   Publisher: _____

   Pages on which information about your country can be found: ___

2. Check your library's *Reader's Guide to Periodical Literature* to find a recent magazine article that discusses some aspect of your country's history, economic situation, political affairs, social issues, cultural background, *or* current events. Record the requested information below:

   Title of periodical: _____

   Issue date: _____

   Pages containing information: _____

3. Ask your librarian for answers to these questions:

   • Can reference books be borrowed?
   • Can periodicals be checked out overnight?
   • Can books and periodicals be photocopied in the library?
   • Where are photocopy machines located in the library and how much does one photocopy cost?

EXTENSION ACTIVITIES

1. Make a list of study habits you intend to develop. Post this list by your desk or bed.

2. Visit your school library and make a list of desk references you might like to have or will probably use frequently in your work at school.

3. Find out about the social organizations on your campus and make a point of attending a meeting of one of these organizations during the next month.

Answers to Exercises

author   _Meilach, Dona Z._   call number _616.73_

title _How to relieve your aching back_

publisher _Bantam_   copyright
                                       date   _1979_

number of pages   _41_   subject
                          heading _1. Backache 2. Exer. therapy_

illustrations? yes: _photographs_ no: _____

Unit 2
Developing Your Vocabulary

● Becoming a Word Collector (Answer Yes or No)

● Using the Dictionary

● Forming Words

If you answered "NO" to any of the questions above, read the indicated pages and do the corresponding exercises.

•Becoming a Word Collector

In order to study in an American university, you need a fairly broad vocabulary of English words. While you are still studying English you can expand and develop your vocabulary in several ways. One way is to become a "word collector" and to write down new words as you encounter them, either through your reading or conversations with others. You can write the words in your notebook in a continuous list, or use 3″ × 5″ index cards. The purpose of the list or card is to help you remember new words by writing them down, reviewing them, and using them from time to time. Look at the word card below:

Side 1   **Side 2**

vocabulary (noun)	The collective words of a language. *Example:* I need to add words to my English <u>vocabulary</u> every day.

Note that the front (side 1) of the card identifies the word and its part of speech. The back (side 2) of the card gives a definition of the word and a sample sentence with the word underlined. The definition of the word may be one that you have heard or learned, or it may come from the dictionary. The sample sentence should be one in which you have actually heard or seen the word used.

 · If you make word cards, like the one above, keep them in alphabetical order and try to review them frequently. Before long, they will become a part of your working vocabulary. And, as your stack of cards or word list grows, notice any similarities among the words and rearrange them according to those similarities, such as subject area, category, and so on.

•Using the Dictionary

Another way to develop your vocabulary is by using your dictionary. There are, of course, many different kinds of dictionaries. But most dictionaries for learners of English are either *bilingual* (with words and definitions given in two languages) or *monolingual* (with words and definitions given in English or another language only). In general, students planning to study in a university where English is the language of instruction should have an English-only dictionary.

A good hardbound English dictionary will offer many features beyond multiple definitions for several thousand words. A good dictionary will indicate how a word is pronounced, what part of speech it is, its plural form or verb endings (inflections), the origin of the word (its etymology), how the word may be used in different contexts, how it is split or hyphenated in writing, and words having the same/similar meaning (synonyms) or an opposite meaning (antonyms) from the main or key word. In addition, many English-only dictionaries contain valuable information regarding the history of the English language, American idioms, slang and colloquial expressions, colleges in the United States (and often Canada), a guide to English punctuation, capitalization, spelling, and abbreviations, forms of address for church officials, public officers, and academic personnel, letter and manuscript writing forms, proofreading instructions and proofreaders' marks, tables of weights and measures, and special signs and symbols.

For practice in evaluating and using your dictionary, turn to *pp. 22–24, exercises 10–12.*

Exercise 10: Dictionary Features

Check your dictionary to see how many of the features below it contains.

Title of dictionary: _____

Publisher: _____

Copyright date: _____

Does your dictionary contain the following?:
- multiple definitions
- pronunciation guide
- part-of-speech labels
- word endings (inflected forms)
- origin of words (etymology)
- separation (hyphenation) marks
- synonyms
- antonyms
- idioms, slang, and colloquial expressions
- abbreviations
- punctuation, capitalization, and spelling guides
- a list of American/Canadian colleges and universities
- forms of address for clergy, public officials, and academic personnel
- letter and manuscript writing forms
- proofreaders' marks
- tables of weights and measures
- special signs and symbols

Exercise 11: Pronunciation and Hyphenation

Look up ten words in your dictionary and write them down on the next page. Be sure you copy the words *exactly* as they appear in your dictionary, complete with pronunciation marks. Then practice pronouncing each word using the marks and information from your dictionary as a guide.

1. _____   6. _____

2. _____   7. _____

3. _____   8. _____

4. _____   9. _____

5. _____   10. _____

Now, using your dictionary, find the words listed below and show how each one can be separated or hyphenated. *Note:* The marks indicating the hyphenation of words in writing are the same as those used to show the pronunciation of syllables (parts of words).

Example: The word *syllable* has three parts: *syl·la·ble* and it may be separated in writing as follows: *syl-la-ble.*

1. energy   _____   6. government _____

2. university _____   7. homework   _____

3. writing   _____   8. language   _____

4. national   _____   9. spelling   _____

5. dictionary _____   10. examination _____

Exercise 12: Dictionary Word Usage

Look up the following key words in your dictionary and write down the different examples of the word as it is used in combination with another word or other words. Then write your own sentences using the word in several different ways.

Example: **have**   have at, have it out, have done, have on, have had it, have to be, have it good, to have and to hold

*I'm tired of cleaning up my room; I've *had it!*

*They're really lucky. They've got lots of money, steady jobs, and a nice home. They *have it good.*

*The little girl *had on* her mother's old dress.

1. give _____

_____

_____

_____

2. look _____

_____

_____

_____

3. put _____

_____

_____

_____

•Forming Words

As you are collecting new words and expanding your English vocabulary by using your dictionary, you may discover that many of the words you are learning begin with the same letters, have the same middle part, or share the same ending. If you have noticed any similarities, you may have been paying attention to how words in English are formed, using affixes and stems. An *affix* is a group of letters that attach to the *stem* (the base form) of a word. If the letters attach to the beginning of the stem, the affix is called a *prefix;* if the letters attach to the end of the stem, the affix is called a *suffix*. Prefixes have meaning of their own and can alter the meaning of a word; suffixes usually change a word's part of speech. Look at the example below.

prefix	stem	suffix
trans-	form	-er
(across)	(form or shape)	noun: one that does something

The prefix *trans-* means *across*, the suffix *-er* refers to a noun and *one that does something*. When both affixes are added to the stem *form*, they create a new word—*transformer*, or something that changes/crosses shape or form.

There are numerous prefixes, suffixes, and stems used in the English language, and it is difficult to learn them all at once. However, you can learn the most common affixes and stems, and with that knowledge you will discover that you know much more vocabulary in English than you thought!

Study the prefixes, stems, and suffixes below. Then turn to *pp. 30–32, exercises 13–14.*

Prefixes

ad-   to, toward; **advance** (to go ahead)

ante-   before; **anteroom** (before the room)

anti-   against, **anti-freeze** (against freezing)

be-   intense; **beloved** (intense love)

bi-   two; **bifold** (two folds)

circum-   around; **circumference** (the area around a circle)

co-, col-, com-, con-   with, together; **co-exist** (to live with), **collect** (to gather together), **computer** (to calculate with), **connect** (to fasten together)

de- away from; **degrade** (to reduce in rank)

dis- take away; not; deprive of; **disregard** (to overlook)

em-, en- in, into; **employ** (to use), **entrap** (to catch in a trap)

e-, ex- out; former; **exit** (to go out); **ex-pilot** (a former pilot)

il-, im-, in-, ir- not; **illegal** (not legal), **improbable** (not probable), **inconsistent** (not consistent); **irrelevant** (not relevant)

im-, in- in; **import** (to bring in from another country), **inhale** (to breathe in)

inter- between, among; **interplay** (play between or among people)

micro- small; **microscope** (an instrument used to make small objects look larger)

mis- badly, poorly; **misunderstand** (to understand poorly)

of- against; **offend** (to act against)

per- throughout; thoroughly, complete; **permeate** (to pass through); **persuade** (to convince completely)

post- after; **postpone** (to put off until later)

pre- before; **prepayment** (payment beforehand)

pro- moving forward or ahead; for; **proceed** (to go forward); **pro-choice** (to be for or in favor of choosing)

re- back; again; **return** (to turn back); **rebuild** (to build again)

sub- under, below; **subway** (a path or way below ground)

syn- same; **synonym** (same name)

trans- across; **transmit** (to send across)

un- not; **unreadable** (not readable)

Stems

alter other; **alternative** (another choice)

anthro man, human; **anthropology** (the study of mankind)

aqua water; **aqueduct** (a large pipe used to carry water from far away)

astro   star; **astronomy** (the science of the stars and planets)

auto   self; **automatic** (self-operating)

bio   life; **biology** (the study of life)

biblio   book, of books; **bibliography** (a list of books)

chron   time; **chronicle** (a historical record arranged in order of time)

cycle   circle; **cyclic** (moving in a circle or cycle)

demo   people; **democracy** (government by the people)

dic, dict   speak or say; **dictate** (to say words aloud)

duc, duct   lead; **conductor** (one who leads)

fac, fact   do or make; **manufacture** (to make by hand or machine)

geo   earth; **geography** (a descriptive science dealing with the earth)

graph   write; **autograph** (one's own writing, signature)

homo   same; **homogeneous** (of the same kind)

hydr   water; **hydrant** (a large pipe connected to a water source)

hyper   extra; **hypersensitive** (extra sensitive)

judic   law; **judicial** (having to do with the law)

liber   free; **liberate** (to free)

logy   study of; **psychology** (the study of the mind or psyche)

manu   hand; **manuscript** (a document written by hand)

mater, matri   mother; **maternal** (motherly), **matricide** (killing of one's mother)

medi   middle; **median** (the middle)

meter   measure; **speedometer** (an instrument that measures speed)

mis, mit   to send; **missile** (something that is sent, thrown, or shot), **remit** (to send back)

mort   death; **mortician** (one who deals with death)

neur   nerve, fiber; **neurology** (the study of the nervous system)

pater   father; **paternity** (fatherhood)

photo light; **photography** (the process of producing images on a light-sensitive surface or film)

phon voice; **telephone** (an instrument that sends and receives the sound of the voice)

port to carry; **transport** (to carry across)

prim first; **primary**

scope to view; **telescope** (an instrument used to view things far away)

scrib, scrip to write; **transcribe,** (to write out in full), **subscription** (to write one's name down for something)

simu same time; **simultaneous** (at the same time)

spec, spect to look; **spectator** (one who watches or looks)

tempo time; **contemporary** (of this time)

ten, tens to stretch, to try; **tension** (the state or condition of being stretched)

tract to pull; **contract** (to pull together)

uni one; **unison** (with one voice)

vene, vent to go, to come; **venture** (an undertaking that comes with danger)

ver true, genuine, **verify** (to prove to be true)

vita life; **vitality** (the power to live)

vid, vis to see; **vision** (the state of being able to see; sight)

Suffixes

-able, -ible (adjective) can do, able; **laughable, lovable, responsible**

-al, -ical, -ial (adjective) belonging to; **verbal, practical, jovial**

-ance, -ence (noun) act of doing; **attendance, independence**

-ant, -ent (noun) acting as agent; **attendant, agent**

-ation (noun) act, state of; **celebration, deliberation**

-ant (adjective) with force; **jubilant**

-er   (noun) one who does; **grower** (adjective), something that is; **smaller**

-est   (adjective) the most; **smartest**

-fic   (adjective) doing, causing; **specific**

-ful   (adjective) full of; **wonderful, joyful**

-fy   (verb) to make, to form; **satisfy, glorify**

-hood   (noun) state, condition; **brotherhood**

-ic   (adjective) one who is; **comic, ecstatic**

-ious, -ous   (adjective) state of being; **glorious, wondrous**

-ish   (adjective) of the nature of; **boyish**

-ist   (noun) one who does; **separatist, colonist**

-ism   (noun) belief or practice of; **elitism, intellectualism**

-ing   (verb) act of doing; **breathing, working**

-ion, -tion   (noun) result of; **precision, combination**

-ity, -ty   (noun) state of being; **intensity, frailty**

-less   (adjective) without, free from, unable; **breathless, merciless**

-ly   (adverb) state of being; **lovely, truthfully**

-ment   (noun) concrete result/thing, manner; **merriment**

-ness   noun from adjective; state of being, condition; **happiness, playfulness**

-ous   (adjective) full of; **beauteous, glorious**

-ship   (noun) state of being, condition; **assistantship, friendship**

-tion   noun from verb; act, state of; **attention**

-ure   (noun) process, act; **adventure**

-y   (adjective) state of being; **happy, funny**

Exercise 13: Recognizing Prefixes and Suffixes

Answer the questions below. Then write a sentence using the same word with the prefix.

1. To *organize* means to put in order.
   What does *disorganized* mean?
   What is a *disorganized* desk?
   Sentence: _____

   _____

2. *Action* means a manner of performing.
   What does *interaction* mean?
   What is *interaction* between two people?
   Sentence: _____

   _____

3. *Related* means connected by a relationship.
   What does *unrelated* mean?
   What does it mean to study *unrelated* subjects?
   Sentence: _____

   _____

4. A *worker* is a person who does a job.
   What is a *co-worker*?
   What does it mean to have a *co-worker* join you on a job?
   Sentence: _____

   _____

5. *Weekly* means every seven days.
   What is *biweekly*?
   What is a *biweekly* newspaper?
   Sentence: _____

   _____

6. *Active* means causing action.
   What does *hyperactive* mean?
   What is a *hyperactive* child?
   Sentence: _____

   _____

7. *Legal* means lawful.
   What does *illegal* mean?
   What is an *illegal* alien?
   Sentence: _____

   _____

8. *Navigate* means to direct the course of a ship.
   What does *circumnavigate* mean?
   What does it mean to *circumnavigate* the world?
   Sentence: _____

   _____

9. *Apartheid* is a system of government that separates black people from
   white.
   What is *anti-apartheid*?
   What does it mean to take an *anti-apartheid* position?
   Sentence: _____

   _____

10. To be *reverent* means to be respectful.
    What does *irreverent* mean?
    What is an *irreverent* student?
    Sentence: _____

    _____

Exercise 14: Using Stems

Using your dictionary and the word stems below, write two examples of words incorporating these stems.

1. **auto**

   _____

2. **phono**

   _____

3. **chron**

   _____

4. **graph**

   _____

5. **scribe**

   _____

6. **geo**

   _____

7. **bio**

   _____

8. **homo**

   _____

9. **philo**

   _____

10. **logy**

    _____

11. **vene**

    _____

12. **miss**

    _____

●Learning Words in Context

Knowing how to use your dictionary and recognizing how words are formed can really help you to develop your vocabulary. However, there is more you can do to increase the number of words you know. You can try to *guess* their meaning from other words around them, or from their context (con = together, with; text = printed words). Sometimes the words surrounding a word will explain that word. Or, the word's meaning may become clear in another sentence. In any case, a word's context is important in terms of understanding its meaning and its function or usage.

To practice identifying words in context, go on to *exercise 15*.

Exercise 15: Recognizing Words in Context

Try to guess the meaning of the words in darker print from their context. Write your guess of each word's meaning in the blanks on the next page. Then check your definitions against those in your dictionary.

Rameshwar Das/Monkmeyer Press

Martin Milford, the **1. architectural designer** enjoyed his work designing homes as well as **2. commercial** buildings. His **3. profession**, which involved his artistic ability, was not the only work he did. Mr. Milford was also a **4. contractor**, whose job it was to make agreements with various **5. tradesmen** to build the structures. He would offer a **6. contract** to the building companies who did the best **7. quality** work at the lowest cost, for he knew that the excellence of their work was worth the price. Some companies, however, who lacked experience in guessing the price of materials, would **8. estimate** their costs to be so high that Mr. Milford would look at them **9. incredulously.** He just couldn't believe the great expense. Very often, after more friendly discussions, an **10. amicable** agreement would be made and the contract would be signed. Mr. Milford experienced great **11. satisfaction** whenever a project was completed. And he was also very pleased when the people for whom he designed and built were **12. contented** with the work.

1. **architectural designer** _____

2. **commercial** _____

3. **profession** _____

4. **contractor** _____

5. **tradesmen** _____

6. **contract** _____

7. **quality** _____

8. **estimate** _____

9. **incredulously** _____

10. **amicable** _____

11. **satisfaction** _____

12. **contented** _____

Study the following list of words and their definitions. By learning the prefixes, stems, and suffixes associated with these words, you will be able to guess the meanings of thousands more English words!

Word	Prefix	Meaning	Stem	Meaning	Suffix	Meaning
intermittent	inter-	between among	mitt	send	-ent	
detain	de-	away from	tain	to have to hold		

Word	Prefix	Meaning	Stem	Meaning	Suffix	Meaning
precept	pre-	before	cept	to take to carry		
offer	of- ob-	against toward	fer	to bear to carry		
insist	in- im-	into	sist	to endure to persist		
monograph	mono-	one	graph	to write		
epilog	epi-	after	log	study speech		
aspect	as- ad- ac-	to toward	spect	to look		
uncomplicated	un-/com- co-	not with	plic	to weave to twist	-ed	past tense
nonextended	non- ex-	not out, from	tend	to stretch	-ed	past tense
reproduction	re-/pro-	back, again for, continue	duct	lead	-tion	condition act of
indisposed	in-/dis- dif-	into not, take away	pos	to place to put	-ed	past tense
oversufficient	over-/suf- under	above, more	fic	to make to do	-ient	
mistranscribe	mis-/trans-	wrong, bad across, through	scribe	to write		

EXTENSION ACTIVITIES

1. Start a collection of word cards (3″ × 5″ index cards). Plan to increase your collection by 15 new cards each week. Review your collection daily and rearrange the cards as new categories and ways of organizing the words suggest themselves.

2. Start a collection of affix cards, indicating the prefix, stem, or suffix of various words. Be sure to include a sample sentence using each word and note its part of speech.

3. Make a card for each of the 14 words listed on pp. 34 and 35. Review the cards frequently until you can recall the prefixes, stems, and suffixes, and the meaning of each word.

Answers to Exercises

Exercise 11 page 23: **1.** en-er-gy **2.** un-i-ver-si-ty **3.** wri-ting **4.** na-tion-al **5.** dic-tion-ar-y **6.** gov-ern-ment **7.** home-work **8.** lan-guage **9.** spel-ling **10.** ex-am-i-na-tion

Exercise 13 page 30: **1.** disorganized = not organized **2.** interaction = action be-tween **3.** unrelated = not related **4.** co-worker = one who works with another **5.** biweekly = every two weeks **6.** hyper-active = very active **7.** illegal = not legal **8.** circumnavigate = sail around **9.** anti-apartheid = against apartheid **10.** irreverent = not reverent

Unit 3
Organizing Your Writing

●Making an Outline (Answer Yes or No)

●Writing a Paragraph

●Writing an Essay

If you answered "NO" to any of the questions above, read the indicated pages and do the corresponding exercises.

•Making an Outline

Of all the skills that you need to be a good student in a university, outlining is one of the most important. Learning how to outline and using that skill in writing, reading, listening, and speaking will enable you to work and study more efficiently. But first you need to know what an outline is.

An outline is a way of organizing ideas or subject matter from the general to the specific. An outline can assist you in several ways. It can help you plan and arrange your ideas before you write; it can help you to understand someone else's ideas in something you read; and it can aid you in following the ideas of someone who is speaking. In short, an outline can help you develop the habit of thinking in categories and learning to use new information effectively.

Ladders of Generality

Another way to think of an outline is to visualize it as a form of step ladder, each step leading down from general to more specific information or ideas. Philosopher/semanticist S.I. Hayakawa introduced the concept of the "abstraction ladder" in his book *Language in Action* (1941), and you will find references to this concept throughout Unit 3. It will be called ladder or steps of generality.

Different Kinds of Outlines

TOPIC OUTLINES

There are basically two kinds of outlines: topic outlines and sentence outlines. With topic outlines, information is arranged in order by topic. For example, look at the list of words below. What is similar about all of them?

lions   tigers   elephants   giraffes

cows   sheep   ducks   chickens

If you answered that they are all names of *animals,* you are right. You could list all of the words under one topic—*animals.*

If you look at the list again, you might notice that not all of the animals are in the same category or class. That is, some are wild animals and some are tame; or some are zoo animals and some are farm animals. So, you could list your animals in two different groups under two separate topic heads as follows:

ANIMALS

Zoo animals	Farm animals
lions	cows
tigers	ducks
elephants	chickens
giraffes	sheep

You could also break these two groups down still further if you wanted, for example, to consider which of the farm animals are mammals and which are fowl. Or you might narrow your topic to consider specific kinds of tigers such as the Bengal, Chinese, or Siberian, or specific types of ducks such as the mallard, canvasback, pintail, or ruddy. In either case, your outline might look something like the ones below.

Animals

  I. **Zoo animals**

  A. **Tigers**

    1. **Bengal**

    2. **Siberian**

  B. **Lions**

  C. **Elephants**

  D. **Giraffes**

 II. **Farm animals**

  A. **Mammals**

    1. **cows**

    2. **sheep**

  B. **Fowl**

    1. **chickens**

    2. **ducks**

Notice the use of Roman numerals (I, II.), arabic numbers (1, 2.) and upper case or capital letters (A, B) in the topic outline above. Notice also the indentation of the numbers and letters from left to right and their vertical alignment. This arrangement is used to indicate movement from more general to specific ideas. Each outline entry or word also begins with the same part of speech, in this case a noun or a noun phrase. Such usage is called *parallelism* and it is an extremely important feature of good outlines.

The same information about animals might also be arranged in step form, as the following "ladder" illustrates:

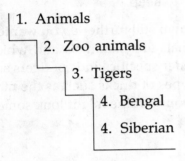

    1. Animals
        2. Zoo animals
            3. Tigers
                4. Bengal
                4. Siberian

In the ladder formation, each numbered step is related to the next numbered step, progressing from general to specific as the numbers increase.

Look at the groups of words below. See if you can arrange the words in each group in stepladder or topic-outline form. You will first need to identify the general group or topic and then arrange the more specific or smaller topics beneath it.

Asia	fingers	Spring	April
Africa	toes	January	March
Continents	head	December	February
Europe	arms	September	October
South America	torso	July	Winter
North America	neck	Fall	May
Australia	legs	Summer	November
Antarctica	hands	June	August
	feet		

The purpose of an outline, or a ladder, is to break down the general group or category into small groups and to classify each group by topic (or sentence). The organization or arrangement of the outlines can assist you later on in studying and recalling information for a special task.

For more practice in making topic outlines, go on to *exercise 16*.

Exercise 16: Topic Outlines

Arrange the following list of words in ladder formation. Then make a topic outline using the basic outline structure provided. Be sure to give your outline a general title.

Jets	DC 8	The *Normandy*
Foreign cars	Transportation	Impala
Cruise ships	Chevrolet	Ships
Cars	Airplanes	Peugeot
American cars	Datsun	Pontiac
Concorde	747	Freight ships
Propeller planes		The *Q.E. II*

Title:

   I.

     A.

       1.

         a.

         b.

　　　　　　　　2.

　　　　　　　　　a.

　　　　　　　　　b.

　　　　　　　　　　　1)

　　　　　B.

　　　　　　　1.

　　　　　　　　a.

　　　　　　　　b.

　　　　　　　　c.

　　　　　　　2.

　　　　　C.

　　　　　　　1.

　　　　　　　　a.

　　　　　　　　b.

　　　　　　　2.

Outline for Exercise 16

   I. Transportation

   A. Cars

      1. Foreign cars

       a. Peugeot

       b. Datsun

      2. American cars

       a. Pontiac

       b. Chevrolet

        1) Impala

Ladder formation

  1. Transportation

    2. Cars

      3. American Cars

       4. Pontiac

       4. Chevrolet

        5. Impala

    B. Airplanes

        1. Jets

           a. DC 8

           b. 747

           c. Concorde

        2. Propeller planes

    C. Ships

        1. Cruise ships

           a. The *Normandy*

           b. The *Q.E. II*

        2. Freight ships

Now, on a separate piece of paper write down a list of items you need to buy at the supermarket. Then arrange the items in topic-outline form using the different areas of the supermarket as your topic heads (Meat, Poultry, Fish, Dairy, Produce, and so on). If you need any help, ask your instructor.

SENTENCE OUTLINES

Sentence outlines are similar to topic outlines except that sentences, rather than key words or topics, are used. A sentence outline also contains more information than a topic outline does, in that it reflects complete thoughts rather than topics or partial ideas. Sentence outlines are particularly useful when you are preparing an oral presentation or need a fairly developed plan before you write a paper.

    Study the following sentence outline prepared by someone preparing a trip.

    We must do several things before we leave on our trip.

      I. First of all, we must talk to our travel agent.

        A. We need flight arrangements and hotel accommodations.

        B. We want to rent a car.

        C. We'd like additional information about places to visit.

II. **Secondly, we need to get appropriate documents and health certificates.**

  A. **We must apply for passports (and visas, if necessary)**

  B. **We must make doctors' appointments for the immunizations we need.**

III. **Thirdly, we'll need to go shopping.**

  A. **We need suitable clothes for a warm climate.**

  B. **We'll want travel items such as guidebooks, maps, medicine, cameras, film, and travel journals.**

  C. **We must have comfortable walking shoes!**

IV. **Finally, we need to make arrangements for our house while we are gone.**

  A. **We need someone to collect our mail and papers.**

  B. **We need someone to water our plants and feed the pets.**

  C. **We might want someone to "house sit" for us.**

Notice that the form of the sentence outline above is the same as that used for the topic outline on p. 41. There is indentation of the numerals, letters and numbers as well as the same vertical alignment. As with the topic outline too, ideas progress from most important (I.), to less important (A., B., C., D.), to the least important, or most specific (1., 2., 3.). As in writing, each sentence is punctuated completely. In addition, transitions such as *First of all, Secondly, Thirdly,* and *Finally,* are used to indicate the sequence of actions to be followed in planning a trip.

  Now read the sentences below and see if you can arrange them in sentence outline form. In some cases you might want to add a transition to a sentence.

Bring the water to a rapid boil.
Take the pasta out of the package or box.
You'll need a 3–4 quart pot.
Add a little salt to the water.
Now you're ready to eat!
Drop the pasta into the boiling water.
Let it cook for about 3 minutes.

You're going to cook pasta.
Fill the pot with cold water.
Drain the pasta in the sink.
Sprinkle a little parsley over everything for a final touch.
Pour it into a large bowl.
Butter the pasta and add a little parmesan cheese.

For more practice in making a sentence outline, go on to *exercise 17.*

Exercise 17: Sentence Outlining

Pretend that you are writing the story of your life—your **autobiography.** First answer the questions below. Then, on a separate piece of paper, arrange your answers in outline form, beginning with the most general information (I., II., III) and following with more specific information (A., B., C., 1., 2., 3, and so on). Use the sample sentence outline on pp. 43 and 44 as a guide, and ask your instructor for help if you need it.

- **What three things do you remember most about your early childhood (ages 3–6)?**

- **What 3 things do you remember about your later childhood (ages 7–12)?**

• **What 3 things do you remember about your teen years (ages 13–19)?**

• **What are some things you have done since you turned 18?**

•Writing a Paragraph

Making an outline is one way to organize your ideas before you write. Whether you choose a topic or a sentence outline, you are establishing a plan of organization that will help you put your words down on paper.

   You may have noticed in your reading, and in this book as well, that most written English is arranged into units or blocks of text called *paragraphs*. A paragraph expresses a main thought or idea that is generally supported by one or more details. Just as the outline from which it may be written, a paragraph begins with the introduction of a topic. In a sentence outline, the first sentence (I.) usually contains the main idea; in a paragraph, the sentence that introduces the main idea is called the *topic sentence* and it is indented. The remaining sentences, in both a sentence outline and a paragraph, are called *supporting sentences* because they contain details that support or control the main idea or topic sentence. The final sentence of a paragraph is called the *concluding sentence*. It restates the main idea or summarizes it in a new way.

   Like the outline that may precede it, a paragraph, according to S.I. Hayakawa, can also be visualized as another kind of ladder—one in which the steps are arranged as follows:

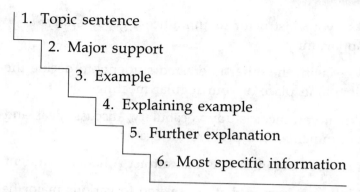

1. Topic sentence
2. Major support
3. Example
4. Explaining example
5. Further explanation
6. Most specific information

Read the sample paragraph below and notice how the main idea and details are arranged.

Interacting with American Students

If you are an international student interested in interacting with American students, try making plans to study in a group and join some campus orgainizations. **First of all,** at the beginning of the term, arrange to study with a group of students in one of your classes. You can do this by asking the instructor to announce to the class a group study opportunity. After that, you can meet with other interested students to decide on the day, time, and place of your regular meetings. When you meet, you can review vocabulary, discuss ideas and assignments, and prepare for exams. **Secondly,** you can join some campus organizations that attract American students. Very often clubs are formed that are related to various major fields and subject areas. These clubs can give you the opportunity to learn more about a subject while hearing English spoken by Americans. A benefit of interacting with Americans in these two ways is that friendships are sometimes formed, even though your primary goal may be to just participate in the language.

Topic sent

Supporting sentence

Concluding sent.

Now see how a sentence outline of the same paragraph looks:

Interacting with American Students

I. International students interested in interacting with American students can do two things.

   A. First of all, at the beginning of the term you can arrange to study with a group of students.

1. Ask your instructor to announce a group study opportunity.

2. Meet with the other interested students to decide the day, time, and place of your regular meetings.

3. When you meet, study vocabulary, discuss ideas and assignments, and prepare for exams.

B. Join campus organizations that attract American students.

1. Clubs are formed that are related to various major fields and subject areas.

2. These clubs can help you to learn more about a subject while allowing you to hear more spoken English.

C. A benefit of forming study groups with Americans and joining campus organizations is that you may make friends, in addition to improving your English.

The diagram* below offers another way to visualize the structure of a paragraph:

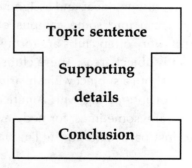

The Topic Sentence

The controlling (or main) idea of a paragraph is found in the topic sentence. The topic sentence is divided into three parts: the subject, the verb, and the controlling idea. The *subject*, or topic, tells the reader what the paragraph is about; the

*Gallo, Joseph and Henry W. Rink, Shaping College Writing: Paragraph and Essay, Fourth Edition, New York: Harcourt Brace Jovanovich, Inc. p. 115.

verb makes a statement about the subject; and the *controlling idea* describes or makes a judgment about the subject. The main function of the controlling idea is to focus or narrow the subject.

Look at the following example:

> The President of the United States is trying to do his best for the country.

In this sentence, *"The President of the United States"* is the subject of the sentence; *is trying* is the verb; and *to do his best for the country* is the controlling idea that needs to be explained or supported by other sentences.

Now look at this sentence:

> The sky is blue.

In this sentence, *The sky* is the subject and *is* is the verb. But where is the controlling idea? Since there is no controlling idea that needs further explanation, it would be difficult to develop a paragraph around this sentence.

For practice in identifying and writing good topic sentences, turn to *p. 50, exercise 18.*

Exercise 18: Topic Sentences

Read the sentences below and check the ones that would make good topic sentences. Be sure that the sentences you choose have controlling ideas. Then try to improve the remaining sentences by adding a controlling idea to each. Follow the example.

_____ **1.** The sky is blue. There are several reasons why the sky appears blue.

_____ **2.** Sometimes it's hard to do homework.

_____ **3.** Study skills are important.

_____ **4.** There are four reasons I want to learn English.

_____ **5.** The students fell asleep in class.

_____ **6.** Our basketball team lost the game.

_____ **7.** There are three separate tests in the TOEFL.

_____ **8.** It was my fault that I failed chemistry last term.

_____ **9.** The computer has changed our lives in many ways.

_____ **10.** The weather is warm.

Now write two topic sentences of your own.

•

•

Supporting Sentences

In addition to a topic sentence, a good paragraph needs supporting sentences that develop the paragraph's main or controlling idea. Read the following paragraph and *underline* the three main sentences that support or control the first or topic sentence.

> The President of the United States is trying to live up to his campaign promises with regard to reducing unemployment, lowering interest rates, and cutting deficits. First of all, he is dealing with the problem of employment. Many more people are employed today than there were when the president was elected. Secondly, the president is trying to lower interest rates. They have dropped from 20 percent to 11 percent in just three years. Last, he is trying to get Congress to lower the deficits.

Notice that two additional sentences—*Many more people are employed today than there were when the president was elected* and *They have dropped from 20 percent to 11 percent in just three years*—add detail to the three main supporting sentences. In this way they, too, support the topic sentence. Notice also the use of certain words and phrases (*First of all, Secondly, Last*) that introduce the supporting sentences. These words and phrases are called **transitions** and will be discussed later on in this unit.

There are various kinds of supporting sentences and each one takes on a specific form. Supporting sentences can be facts or proof to support a claim; they can be quotations given inside quotation marks (" "); they can describe the topic sentence; or they can relate personal experiences or the experiences of others. Their main function, however, is to support the controlling idea of the topic sentence by adding further information and details.

For practice in developing supporting sentences, turn to *p. 52, exercise 19.*

Exercise 19: Supporting Sentences

Select *one* of the two sentences you wrote for Exercise 18 (Topic sentences) and develop it with supporting sentences. Refer to the model paragraphs on p. 47 and p. 51 for guidance.

Transitions

A paragraph must have a main or controlling idea that is introduced by a topic sentence and supported by several other sentences that contribute additional details. However, supporting sentences alone will not hold a paragraph together. Like a sandwich without spreads to hold the filling and two pieces of bread together, a paragraph needs some words or phrases to hold its topic, supporting, and concluding sentences together. Words or phrases used to tie a paragraph's sentences together and to give the paragraph *coherence*, are called *transitions*. Read the following paragraph that lacks transitions. Notice how choppy or uneven the sentences are.

Sami decided to organize a picnic. He called his friends. He went to the supermarket. He bought hot dogs. He bought potato salad. He bought lemonade and soda to drink. He went home. He waited for his friends to come over. They all went to the city park. They played soccer. They grilled the hot dogs. They ate. They cleaned up and went for a walk around the park. They went home at sundown. They enjoyed themselves. Sami had a good idea.

Jose Carrillo/Stock, Boston

Now read the paragraph below. Notice how smooth and coherent it is with the use of transitions to link the sentences together.

> *One day* Sami decided to organize a picnic. *First,* he called his friends. *Next,* he went to the supermarket to buy some hot dogs, potato salad, and lemonade and soda to drink. *Then* he went home and waited for his friends to come over. *When* they arrived, they all went to the city park and played soccer. *After* the game, they grilled the hot dogs and ate. *Then* they cleaned up and went for a walk around the park. *At sundown,* after they had enjoyed themselves, they went home. Sami certainly had a good idea for the day!

Listed below are some common transitional devices grouped in categories. Study the lists carefully and notice how these transitions are used when you encounter them in your reading.

Addition	Result	Conclusion/Summary
and	therefore	last
or	consequently	finally
nor	accordingly	lastly
also	hence	in conclusion
in addition	thus	to conclude
again	for this reason	to summarize
first, second, etc.	truly	in summary
besides	as a result	to sum up
further	then	in brief
furthermore	in short	in short
next		on the whole
moreover		
equally important		

Contrast	Emphasis	Passage of Time
but	in fact	afterwards
on the other hand	indeed	at length
after all	in any event	immediately
however	more important	in the meantime
nevertheless	most important	meanwhile

Contrast

on the contrary
still
yet
notwithstanding
at the same time
in spite of the fact that
for all that
although true
in contrast

Emphasis

specifically
in particular

Passage of Time

soon
after a short time
while
thereupon
thereafter
temporarily
until
presently

Example

for example
for instance
in this manner
that is

Comparison

in the same way
likewise
similarly

Concession

of course
after all
naturally
although this may be true
I admit

Place

here
beyond
opposite to
on the opposite side
above
below
beside
in the distance
adjacent to
there
shortly
since
later

Purpose

for this reason
to this end
with this purpose

For practice using transitions, turn to *p. 56, exercise 20.*

Thanks to Raymond S. Henry, The University of Toledo Community and Technical College, Communications Dept., 1976, for creating this list.

Exercise 20: Using Transitions

Read the paragraph below and insert appropriate transitions to make the paragraph more coherent. Review the model paragraph on p. 54 if you need help.

> Of all my neighbors, Nosy Nora is the most exasperating because of her constant snooping. She looks in other people's windows, and then jumps to the wrong conclusions. Last Saturday afternoon, while looking through her telescope into Ed's apartment window, Nora saw blood all over the kitchen floor. She was convinced that someone had been murdered in Ed's apartment. She called the police. Ed had gone hunting that morning and had been cleaning rabbits on the kitchen floor. Nosy Nora observes the arrivals and departures of people in her building and makes unjust judgments about their conduct. Nora said that Joan was a "bad woman" because she "stayed out all night," arriving home at 8 A.M. every morning last week. Joan is a private duty nurse who was working late at the hospital. Nosy Nora deserves the name "nosy." Her snooping is becoming a nuisance!

Thanks to Judith Hanaken, Ph.D., The University of Toledo Community and Technical College, Communications Dept., 1976, for creating the original Nosy Nora paragraph.

The Concluding Sentence

Many paragraphs contain a summarizing statement or a concluding sentence, but not all do. Paragraphs that are part of the introduction (beginning) or the body (middle) of an essay or a piece of writing several paragraphs long, may not contain a specific conclusion. However, single paragraphs or paragraphs that form the actual conclusion of an essay or a longer piece of writing generally include a summarizing sentence or two to tie up or restate the main idea of that paragraph or essay.

Look at the paragraph below and notice how the concluding sentence relates to the main idea expressed in the first, or topic sentence.

> The brain is a large organ, about the size of a grapefruit, that has two parts. One part, the left side, houses the neurons and synapses that allow us to process cognitive information. The right side has neurons and synapses that trigger our creative energies and abilities. Put very

simply, the brain is a living organ that can grow and change and store information that has been organized and synthesized for recall at a later time. It is a complicated and most remarkable storage and retrieval system whose synapses can expand and grow as we add new experience. However, it has been said by many scientists that the average human being only uses 8 percent of his or her brain. Just think how easily we might solve all of the problems of the world, if we only learned how to use this essential part of our bodies more fully!

Concluding sentence

Adapted from R. Ornstein and R.F. Thompson, *The Amazing Brain,* (Boston: Houghton Mifflin Co., 1984).

For practice in writing a paragraph complete with topic, supporting, and concluding sentences, turn to *p. 58, exercise 21.*

Exercise 21: Writing a Paragraph

Using the sentences you wrote for exercises 18 and 19, write a coherent paragraph. Be sure to attach appropriate transitions to your supporting sentences, and include a summarizing statement as a conclusion.

•Writing an Essay

Most of the writing you do in college or university will be more than one paragraph in length. And most of that writing will be *expository* writing; that is, writing that is used to show or to explain your—or someone else's—ideas or thoughts about a particular topic or subject. Such writing, found in most of your textbooks, is most often required of students for essay exams, compositions, or research papers, and for in-class writing. Other styles of writing—descriptive (describing people, places, things) and narrative (telling a story or relating an event)—though used, are less common in university course work.

Thesis Statements

An essay is a form of expository writing consisting of more than one paragraph. Like a paragraph, an essay has a **beginning**, a **middle**, and an **end**. The beginning, or introduction, may be one or more paragraphs in length and it contains a *thesis statement*, or a statement of the main idea of the essay. The thesis statement of an essay is more complex than the topic sentence of a paragraph because a thesis statement contains ideas and words (topic controls) that will be developed into topic sentences for the subsequent paragraphs in the essay.

Look at the essay that follows and notice how the different parts of the italicized thesis statement, in paragraph 1, form part of the topic sentences for paragraphs 2 and 3. Notice also the other divisions of the essay: the body (supporting paragraphs) and conclusion.

Administrative and Managerial Occupations*

thesis

Managers and administrators achieve organizational objectives by planning and directing the activities of others. In a very small enterprise, the owner may also be the manager. However, as a business or other organization grows and becomes more complex, more people are needed to oversee the operations of the work force. Large corporations or government agencies may employ hundreds of managers, organized into a hierarchy of administrative positions.

Introduction

Top level managers—executives—are primarily concerned with policy making, planning, and overall coordination. They direct the activities of

Occupational Outlook Handbook, U.S. Department of Labor, Bureau of Statistics, Bulletin 2200, 17, U.S.C. #403, 1982–83 edition.

the organization through departmental or mid-level managers. Top level managers include school superintendents, police and fire chiefs, bank presidents, governors, mayors, hospital administrators, chief executive officers of corporations, department store managers, and government agency directors. Below the top management in a large organization are the middle managers who direct various departments. Middle managers may handle a particular area, such as personnel, accounting, sales, finance, or marketing. Or they may supervise the production process at a factory or industrial plant. Middle managers are the people who keep things running smoothly. They organize activities at the operating level and provide direct supervision.

Middle managers work with the assistance of support personnel who plan, organize, analyze, and monitor activities. Support personnel include accountants, loan officers, employment interviewers, purchasing agents, and inspectors of all kinds. Jobs such as these require technical expertise or a thorough understanding of a particular procedure or operation.

Managers and administrators are employed in virtually every type of industrial plant, commercial enterprise, and government agency. Large numbers are employed in finance, insurance, real estate, construction, public administration, health, education, transportation, and public utilities.

Now read the following essay describing "engineering challenges" and see if you can identify—by *underlining*—the thesis statement and the topic sentences of each of the six supporting paragraphs.

Engineering Challenges*

If engineers are problem solvers, then what are the problems? Some have been inherited from past generations; others are consequences of solutions to previous problems; and some are starting to surface that threaten our quality of living. Only an overview of a few of the major concerns are identified in this essay.

The depletion of our petroleum is a serious problem. The total impact of the earth's dwindling fuel tank is affecting our economic stability, defense, employment, productivity, recreation, and social atti-

*Thomas Blotter, *Introduction to Engineering* (New York: John Wiley & Sons, 1981), pp. 9–14.

tudes. The human muscle that pulled the handcarts of westward migration in the 1850s has been conveniently replaced with engines mounted in automobiles, trucks, and airplanes for the 1980s. An automobile industry based on the availability of gasoline constitutes 10 percent of our gross national product (GNP), and is responsible for over 13 million jobs or about one sixth of the total U.S. employment. The economy withstood the abandonment of the handcarts, but could we survive the loss of the combustion engine? Society is depending on engineers and other members of the technology team to provide continued transportation.

The production of food is a problem. In the United States, less than 6 percent of the working population is required to produce the food required. In some underdeveloped countries, at least three out of four individuals are involved in the pursuit of food, and yet many starve. American agriculture is a champion in the area of productivity, yet the challenge continues. Arid lands need to be brought under cultivation as the increasing population of the world absorbs more space. Irrigation systems must be designed and built. Some agricultural machines are almost unbelievable, such as the hay stacker, which harvests over 3,000 bales per day untouched by human hands. Yet, better machines to harvest fruit, vegetables, and animal feeds must become available. Processing food, eliminating waste, efficient storing, packaging, and distributing food are in need of improved technology. The American public pays a lower percentage of their income for food than any other country and expects the bonanza to continue.

The protection of our precious environment is a problem. The natural filtering phenomena provided by our ecological system cannot process the tons of waste that it receives continuously. Technology must provide waste disposal systems. As our population increases and space becomes more critical, we cannot simply haul our garbage away to some isolated location. Moreover, our streams, rivers, and lakes cannot absorb unlimited amounts of sewage and industrial waste. What is needed now are better sewage treatment plants, whereby the outflow is then returned to the natural streams. Ultimately, further technology in the area of particle separators, electrostatic precipitators, polarizers, catalytic converters, sewage disposal systems, purifiers, scrubbers, and other systems must be developed to maintain our ecology, yet allow the required productivity.

Space exploration is a challenge of the future. As our generation reaps the rewards of sacrifices made by early explorers that opened new regions of the earth, we must continue these efforts and unlock the mysteries of outer space. Prior explorations have resulted in multi-dimensional improvements in our standard of living. In a similar way, space technology inundates the space program to enrich our quality of life. Many spin-offs from space technology, such as the voice-controlled wheelchair, are found in home design, brain surgery, cancer treatment, fire prevention, food products, pollution control, airlines, energy systems, heart pacers, and many others. Indeed, space technology is helping to solve many of our domestic problems.

There are many other problems that need engineering solutions. Transportation systems, medical equipment, human transplants, dams, computers, and other challenges await the scrutiny of engineers.

When you have finished reading and marking the essay, "Engineering Challenges," go on to *exercise 22.*

Exercise 22: Writing Thesis Statements

Look at the topics below and write an appropriate thesis statement for an essay about each one. Be sure to include details (topic controls) that can be used to write topic sentences for the supporting paragraphs of the essay.

1. Three Things I Want Other Students to Know About My Country (or Family)

2. Why I Selected This University in the United States (or any other country)

3. The Things I Have Found Most Interesting About the United States (or any other country you have visited)

Supporting Paragraphs

Just as the supporting sentences of a paragraph act as the "filling" between the top slice of bread (the topic sentence) and the bottom slice (the concluding sentence), the supporting paragraphs of an essay serve as the body of the essay, linking its introduction and conclusion. And just as the paragraph uses transitions to hold its supporting sentences together, to give a paragraph coherence, an essay uses transitions to connect its supporting paragraphs. In fact, an essay may include an entire paragraph as a transition from one idea or argument to another. The supporting paragraphs of an essay, or the body of the essay, are the place where the writer develops his ideas.

Look back at the essay "Engineering Challenges," on pp. 60–62. Note how the topic sentences you underlined introduce four paragraphs that identify and describe the "problems" cited in the introduction or first paragraph of the essay. These four paragraphs develop the writer's overview of engineers' concerns.

Conclusions

As with paragraphs containing a final or concluding sentence, essays generally include a final paragraph or **conclusion** that contains a topic and supporting sentences just like any other paragraph. The conclusion serves the same purpose too, to summarize or tie up the general argument or idea of the essay. It is not the place to introduce a new or unusual idea. Some conclusions may begin or end with a question for the reader to ponder. But the question usually relates to the main or general idea of the essay as a whole.

Look back again at the essay "Engineering Challenges," on pp. 60–62 and study the final paragraph. Note how the writer reviews other problems that engineers face while keeping to the general topic.

Now turn to *p. 64, exercise 23* for practice in writing the body of the essay you began in exercises 21–22.

Exercise 23: Developing Supporting Paragraphs

Using *one* of the thesis statements you wrote in Exercise 22, develop an essay of several paragraphs. Begin by writing topic sentences for each of the paragraphs you intend to write. Don't forget to include transitions, when appropriate, and to finish with a concluding paragraph.

If you have read this unit carefully and have done all of the exercises, you should be able to write an essay of several paragraphs in length, including a thesis statement, supporting paragraphs, and a conclusion.

To see how well you organized the essay you wrote in Exercise 23, turn to *p. 66, exercise 24.*

Exercise 24: Outlining an Essay

In the space below, prepare a topic or sentence outline of the essay you wrote in Exercise 23. Be sure to indent and to include the appropriate Roman numerals (I., II., III.) to indicate the most important ideas, and capital letters (A., B., C.), arabic numbers (1., 2., 3.), and lower-case letters (a., b., c.) to indicate ideas of decreasing importance.

Extension Activities

1. Work with another student or a small group. Brainstorm a topic together, such as different kinds of music you like or different singers. Then arrange your ideas in *topic outline* form.

2. Explain to someone else how to make or do something (for example, how to fry an egg or how to type a paper). Then, write each of the steps down in *sentence outline* form.

3. Interview your teacher or a classmate. Ask four or five general questions and write down the person's replies to each. Then, organize the answers into sentences in a paragraph. Be sure you include a topic sentence and appropriate transitions to link each of the sentences together.

Answers to Exercises
Exercise 18 p. 50: The following sentences need further development (controlling ideas) to become good topic sentences: **1., 2., 3., 5., 6., 10.** *pp. 60–62* The thesis sentence of "Engineering Challenges" is: *If engineers are problem solvers, then what are the problems?* The topic sentences of the four supporting paragraphs are: **1.** *The depletion of our petroleum is a serious problem.* **2.** *The production of food is a problem.* **3.** *The protection of our precious environment is a problem.* **4.** *Space exploration is a challenge of the future.*

Note to the Student:
Before you begin the next Unit, you will need to get a textbook that you will be using next term. You can get it from the library, college book store, or from a friend.

Unit 4
Improving Your Reading

*If you answered "NO" to any of the questions above, read the indicated pages and
do the corresponding exercises.*

●Previewing a Textbook

When you begin your university course work, even when you are studying English, you will need to buy certain textbooks for your classes. These books will help you build your knowledge in a particular subject area or field.

Although reading several textbooks, or even one, in a language that is not your own can seem an overwhelming task at times, there are ways to make that task easier. One way is to survey or *preview* (pre- = ahead, view = look at) your textbook.

Look at the list of words and phrases below that describe features and sections of a typical course textbook and their order of appearance (from front to back of the book). You may recognize some of the terms from the library vocabulary discussed in Unit 1.

Title – the name of the book

Subtitle – a second name that appears after or under the book's title (usually in smaller type)

Author(s) – the person or persons who wrote the book

Copyright date – the year in which the book was first issued; this date appears on the back of the first page containing the title and author of the book

Table of Contents (or Contents) – the section at the front of the book that tells what the book contains and on which pages

Introduction or Preface – the opening chapter of the book, in which the author explains his or her purpose in writing the book, how it is organized, and how it can be used

Unit, Chapter, or Section opening – the first page of a unit, chapter, or section of a book

Text head(s) and subhead(s) – a brief phrase that introduces a portion of a reading text; usually printed in darker, larger print

Footnotes – numbered notes at the bottom, or foot, of the page indicating where certain information is from

References – the titles, authors, and publication information about books used in preparation of the actual textbook

Questions – questions for writing or discussion, usually at the end of a chapter, dealing with the chapter's content

Summary – one or several paragraphs at the end of a chapter, reviewing the most important information in the chapter

Glossary – an alphabetical listing of words, terms, and unfamiliar vocabulary appearing in the text

Appendix (or Appendices) – additional material, exercises, answer keys, and so on, appearing at the end of a textbook

Bibliography – a list of books, alphabetically arranged, indicating all of the works referred to in the preparation of a book

Index – an alphabetical directory of subject matter and specific topics covered in a book

Not every textbook has *all* of the indicated features or sections, but many do. Look through this textbook—*Language and Study Skills for Learners of English*—now and check how many of the listed sections or features it contains. Be sure to study the Contents pages carefully for an overview of the entire book.

As part of your textbook preview, try to formulate questions about the text (what is written) and to predict answers about the information provided. Being able to make predictions about written material can help you improve your reading skills and make you a better reader.

For more practice in previewing textbooks, turn to *p. 72, exercise 25*. You will need to have a textbook (with expository writing) that you will be using in a course next term for some of the following exercises.

Exercise 25: Previewing a Textbook

Preview one of your course textbooks for next term using the following form.

Title:

Subtitle (if any):

Author(s):

Publisher:

Copyright date:

Introduction or Preface: pages _____ to _____

Contents

   List three sections or unit headings:

   1.

   2.

   3.

   List three chapter headings:

   1.

   2.

   3.

   Write three questions based on the section or chapter headings:

   1.

   2.

   3.

Glossary

   Approximately what percentage of the words or terms look unfamiliar to you (10%–100%)? _____

Index

   Is there an *author index* as well as a subject or topic index?

References

List three books that might give you additional information:

1. **Title:**
   Author:

2. **Title:**
   Author:

3. **Title:**
   Author:

Check which of the following appear in your book:

Footnotes? _____   **Bibliography?** _____

End-of-chapter questions? _____

End-of-chapter activities? _____

Chapter summaries? _____

After previewing an entire textbook, preview the introduction or preface. The introductory portion of a book can give you an overview of the book or author's main idea(s) and intent. Next, preview the first chapter of the book. Be sure to note the chapter headings and any information appearing in photos, artwork, tables, or other graphic aids on the pages. If the chapter includes a summary, read it. The summary will review the important points of the chapter. Finally, to make your preview an active, rather than a passive process, turn the chapter titles and headings into questions.

•Skimming

"Opening your brain to new ideas can give you a real headache."

Once you have previewed a textbook, the introduction, and/or the first chapter, you have a fairly good idea about what the book contains and the topics it will cover. You are now ready to do some closer reading. However, before you begin, you need to know about *skimming*. Skimming is a way of reading for the general or main idea of a text. When you skim a textbook, you do not read every single word. Reading word-by-word slows you down and often reduces your overall comprehension.

In skimming, you quickly read the title or heading (if there is one) of the text and the first sentence of each paragraph (if there is only one) or the last paragraph—the conclusion—of the text. By reading only the first and last portions of the text, you are again "previewing" the text to get a general idea of its content. You are *not* reading for details or for specific information.

Skim the following paragraphs and decide which of the sentences best expresses the main idea of that paragraph:

Paragraph 1

It would not be wise to make a trip to study in the United States without some advance planning. First of all, you need to apply to a university and be accepted. As part of the application process, you will have to send your secondary school transcript, letters of recommendation, and a statement of your family's financial status. You might also need to write an essay on why you want to study at the university to which you are applying. Next, if your application is accepted, you will need to get a passport and/or a visa and make appropriate housing arrangements. Usually, the university accepting you will offer some housing opportunities and advice. But you might have to do a lot of investigating yourself. Once you have arrived at the university, you will have to go through registration and become familiar with your new environment. You will need to acquire a good map of your city and campus and to make sure of the dates and times for registering for classes. You will also want to find out about ways to meet people on campus, social organizations, and other activities. In other words, before you even set foot in a university classroom in the United States, you have to go through a major organizational process that requires step-by-step planning.

The main idea of Paragraph 1 is:
a) Studying in the United States is difficult.
b) Studying in the United States requires advance planning.
c) You need many documents in order to study in the United States.
d) You need to register before you attend classes in the United States.

Paragraph 2

An excellent formula for learning the material in a textbook is referred to as *PQ5R*. the *P* stands for *preview,* to look at the material and to raise questions about it. The *Q* means to *question* as you read, trying to guess or to predict what the text is about. The 5 *R*s are *read, reflect* (think about), *record* (write down), *recite* (say aloud), and *review* (go over again and again). Knowing the PQ5R formula can make studying college textbooks easier.

The main idea of Paragraph 2 is:
a) You should question what you read.
b) Learning the 5 Rs can make you a better reader.

    c) PQ5R is a formula to help you read textbooks.
    d) Previewing your textbook is a good idea.

Adapted from Francis P. Robinson, *Effective Reading* (New York: Harper & Row, 1962), pp. 31–33.

Now open this textbook to the introduction. Skim the introduction and try to determine the main idea. You might apply the *PQ5R formula* as you skim the pages. Question what you read and be sure to reflect, or think about, the content. Then write below what you think the main idea of the introduction is:

For more practice in skimming, go on to *exercise 26.*

Exercise 26: Skimming

Using one of your course textbooks, skim the introduction or preface and answer the following questions:

Title of textbook:

Publisher:

Introduction or Preface: **pages** _____ **to** _____

    1. What is the main idea of paragraph 1?

_____

_____

_____

2. What is the author's conclusion (last paragraph)? Try to write it *in your own words*.

_____

_____

_____

3. What are some other things you learned from reading the introduction or preface?

_____

_____

_____

•Scanning

Another skill that will help you improve your reading is **scanning**. Unlike skimming, which involves rapid reading for the main idea, scanning calls for reading for specific information or details. In skimming, you read quickly and then pose questions and make predictions about a text's content. In scanning, you generally have a specific question or idea already in mind; you scan the text to find particular information to answer your question or to confirm your idea. For example, if you wanted to know which chapter of your American history book contained information about recovery following the Civil War, you would *scan* the Contents to locate the chapter dealing with the Civil War (1861–1865) and the pages of that chapter covering the years following the war (1865 on).

Scanning is most easily done when the information you need is given in numerical lists or the names of people, places, and things appear in boldface print. However, you can also scan for words and phrases that will answer a particular question.

Read the questions below; then scan the following paragraphs for the answers.

1. In what year did the stock market crash?

The period from 1917 to 1929 saw a new beginning for people in the U.S. there were technological inventions such as the airplane and the automobile. World War I was fought in Europe and was known as "the war to end all wars." It was supposed to have brought peace to the world. The "Roaring Twenties" was a time of social change with a booming economy that ended in the crash of the stock market in 1929.

2. What problems were *not* addressed during the 1980s?

The 1980s brought increased technological advances as the age of the computer was firmly established. Inflation was curbed somewhat, but the rise in unemployment continued to be a major problem. Though world tensions and the armament race were at dangerous levels, the American people reelected genial, affable Ronald Reagan as president for a second term. The real problems of how the peoples of the world could begin to understand each other and get along in peaceful coexistence were yet to be addressed.

Now that you've learned about both skimming and scanning, *scan* the introduction of this book for answers to these questions:

1. For whom is this book intended?

    _____

2. Where can it be used? (in what classroom situations)

    _____

3. How can it be used?

    _____

For additional scanning practice, go on to *exercise 27.*

Exercise 27: Scanning

Using one of your course textbooks, scan the Contents to locate the page numbers of a particular chapter you need, or would like, to read. Then, turn to that chapter and look for answers to the following questions.

1. What important people or places are mentioned on the first page of the chapter?

   _____

   _____

   _____

2. What dates or events are mentioned on the second page of the chapter?

   _____

   _____

   _____

3. What information can you find in an illustration (photo, drawing, graph, or table) on the third page of the chapter?

   _____

   _____

   _____

4. What other specific information can you learn from scanning the rest of the chapter?

   _____

   _____

   _____

•Using Graphic Aids

As part of learning to preview a textbook, you looked at the illustrations and other graphic information that appeared with the text. And, in scanning for specific information in Exercise 27, you may have found answers in the graphic information presented in your textbook. Graphic information can be found in pictures, tables, charts, maps, lists of figures, and other illustrations. The purpose of such graphic aids is to enhance the meaning of the printed text and/or to convey meaning in another way.

Study the following graphs and note the kind of information each one gives. Be sure to read the title or caption for each graph. The first group of graphs are line graphs, the second group are bar graphs, and the third group are circle or pie graphs. Another kind of graph, a pictograph, is illustrated on p. 85.

Line Graphs

A line graph shows the relationship between two variables. It has a vertical axis which represents one variable and a horizontal axis which represents the other. The statistics are recorded by plotting (placing) a point (a dot) where the two variables cross. For example, on the next page is a line graph that illustrates the grade point averages (GPA) of the five international students in an engineering class at State University.

As you can see, the **vertical axis** illustrates the **grade point average** while the **horizontal axis** represents **student number**. Each dot, or **plotted point**, shows the GPA for each particular student. Student #5 had a 3.9 GPA since the **plotted point** is just below the 4.0 line. Student #2 has a 2.1.

GRAPH A—Line Graph

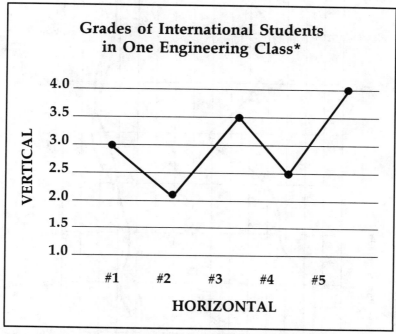

**Grades of International Students
in One Engineering Class***

*Source: State University, June, 1991. Student Records.

1. What kind of graph is this? _____

2. What does it measure? _____

3. What does each horizontal line represent? _____
_____

4. What does each vertical line represent? _____
_____

5. What does each point on the graph represent? _____
_____

6. Which student received the highest grade? _____

7. Which student received the lowest grade? _____

8. What was the average grade of all five students? _____

Graph B—Multiple Line Graph

Commodity Shipments (in tons): Port of Toledo

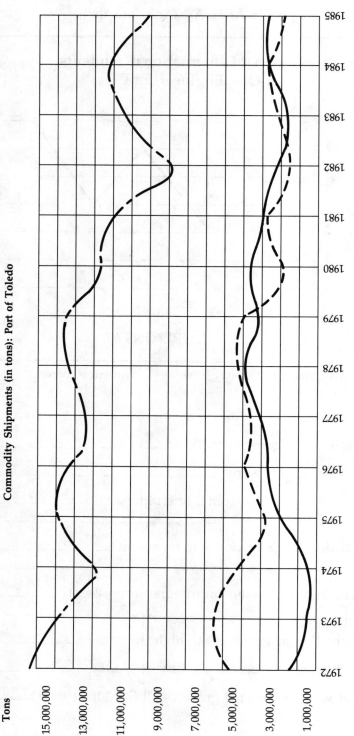

Coal —————
Iron ore — — —
Grain —————

Source: Toledo-Lucas County Port Authority, Toledo, Ohio.

This is a **multiple line graph** that depicts the records of three different commodities: coal, iron ore, and grain. Preview the questions, study the graph, and then answer the questions below.

1. Each line on the horizontal axis represents _____
   _____

2. Each line on the vertical axis represents _____
   _____

3. How are the three different commodities represented? _____
   _____

4. What does each plotted point represent? _____
   _____

5. In which year was the greatest amount of coal shipped? _____
   The least? _____

6. In 1983 the number of tons of coal shipped was _____ times the number of tons of grain.

As you can readily see, the example given for the line graph could have been represented in bars just as the line-graph *A* is represented in vertical bars in Graph *C*.

Bar Graphs

Bar graphs are similar to line graphs and the statistician often has a choice of using one or the other to illustrate the figures. The only difference is that bars are used to illustrate those figures rather than lines. As an example, look at the same figures that represent the grades of international students at State University that appeared on a line graph A on page 81 and see how it looks illustrated in bars.

Graph C—Bar Graph

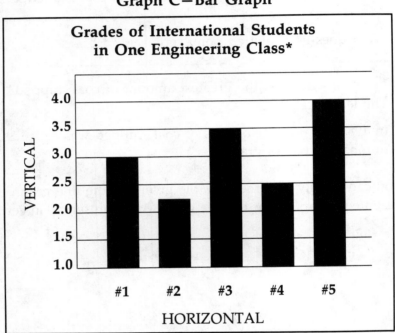

*Source: State University, June, 1991. Student Records.

1. What kind of graph is this? _____

   _____

2. What does it measure? _____

   _____

3. What does each horizontal line represent? _____

   _____

4. What does each vertical line represent? _____

   _____

5. What does each point on the graph represent? _____

_____

6. Which student received the highest grade? _____

_____

7. Which student received the lowest grade? _____

_____

8. What was the average grade of all five students? _____

_____

Graph D—Pictograph

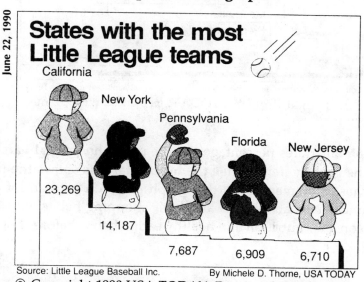

June 22, 1990

States with the most Little League teams

California

New York

Pennsylvania

Florida

New Jersey

23,269

14,187

7,687

6,909

6,710

Source: Little League Baseball Inc.   By Michele D. Thorne, USA TODAY

© Copyright 1990 USA TODAY. Reprinted with permission.

This is actually a **vertical bar graph** that illustrates the information by using **pictures** rather than **vertical bars**. It is called a **pictograph**. Based on the information, list some assumptions about why California has the most Little League baseball teams.

1. _____

2. _____

3. _____

4. _____

Graph E—Horizontal Bar Pictograph

Source: Opinion Research Corporation   By Jeff Dionise, USA TODAY

© Copyright 1990 USA TODAY. Reprinted with permission.

This **pictograph** illustrates percentages by the use of **horizontal bars**. The **vertical axis** lists the grocery items while the **horizontal axis** shows the percentages of items purchased by men. Does this graph give you enough information to draw some conclusions about men and their shopping habits? List three ways that men can consider nutrition and healthy eating habits before shopping in the future.

1. _____

2. _____

3. _____

Pie or Circle Graphs

In a circle graph, or Pie chart, the statistician uses a circular region to illustrate the total of all the information to be communicated. The circle is divided into sections in order to show the divisions as percentages of the entire circle. Just as in the line and bar graph, you will need to read the caption, or title, carefully in addition to noting the segments of the circle. Then you will have to study the graph in order to see relationships and raise questions. The example that follows illustrates how a circle graph can be divided.

Graph F—Circle Graph or Pie Chart

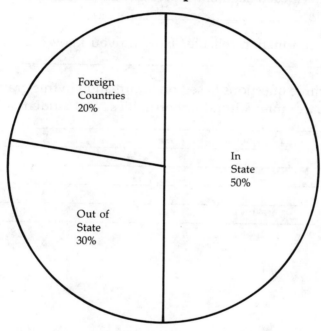

Foreign
Countries
20%

In
State
50%

Out of
State
30%

STUDENT BODY AT STATE UNIVERSITY

1. What percentage of the students at State University come from foreign countries?

2. What percentage of students are from in state?

Statistics, or groups of numbers and percentages, either printed in a text or appearing in tables, graphs, and charts are often used to support other information in the reading text. When interpreting graphic aids, it is important to note the date and source of the information, as well as any explanatory notes that accompany the aid.

For practice in "reading" graphic aids, turn to *p. 88, exercise 28.*

Exercise 28: Reading Graphs

Graph F: Student Body at State University (p. 87)

1. What kind of graph is this? _____

_____

2. What does the entire circular region represent? _____

_____

3. What does each segment represent? _____

_____

4. Is this information reliable? How do you know? _____

_____

5. Write three questions based on information in this graph as to dormitory space, intercultural opportunities, and student advising.

a. _____

_____

b. _____

_____

c. _____

_____

Graph G—Line Graph

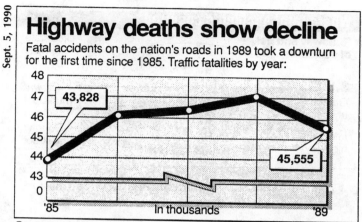

Sept. 5, 1990

Highway deaths show decline

Fatal accidents on the nation's roads in 1989 took a downturn for the first time since 1985. Traffic fatalities by year:

43,828

45,555

In thousands

Source: National Highway Traffic Administration. By Keith Carter, USA TODAY © Copyright USA TODAY. Reprinted with permission.

1. What kind of graph is this? _____

2. What does it measure? _____

3. Each line on the horizontal axis represents _____
   _____

4. Each line on the vertical axis represents _____
   _____

5. What does each plotted point represent? _____
   _____

6. Which year had the most highway deaths? _____
   _____

7. What does each interval represent? _____
   _____

Graph H—Circle Graph

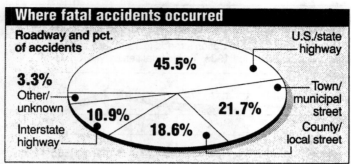

Where fatal accidents occurred

Roadway and pct. of accidents

U.S./state highway

45.5%

3.3%
Other/unknown

Town/municipal street

21.7%

10.9%

Interstate highway

18.6%

County/local street

Source: National Highway Traffic Safety Administration   By Keith Carter, USA TODAY

© Copyright USA TODAY. Reprinted with permission.

1. What kind of graph is this? _____

2. What does it measure? _____

3. Where did most accidents occur? _____

4. What is the source of the information? _____

   Is it reliable? _____

5. Draw some conclusions for yourself, as well as other students, after studying this graph.

   _____

   _____

   _____

   _____

   _____

Graph I

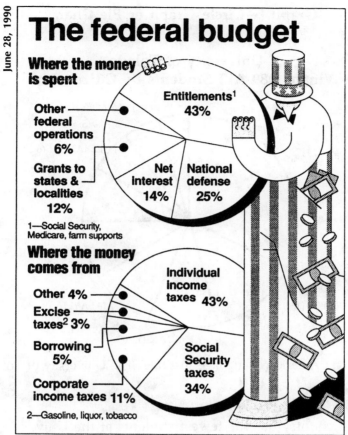

June 28, 1990

The federal budget

Where the money is spent

- Other federal operations 6%
- Grants to states & localities 12%
- Net interest 14%
- Entitlements[1] 43%
- National defense 25%

1—Social Security, Medicare, farm supports

Where the money comes from

- Other 4%
- Excise taxes[2] 3%
- Borrowing 5%
- Corporate income taxes 11%
- Individual income taxes 43%
- Social Security taxes 34%

2—Gasoline, liquor, tobacco

Source: White House Budget Office   By Keith Carter, USA TODAY

1. What kind of graphs are these? _____

2. What do they measure? _____

3. What does the entire circular region represent? _____

4. What are entitlements? _____

5. What are Excise Taxes? _____

6. What is the source of the information? Is it reliable? _____

7. Write three questions that these graphs might suggest.

   a. _____

   b. _____

   c. _____

Graph J—Circle Graph or Pie Chart

University of Toledo
Winter 1989 ALI Students by Citizenship

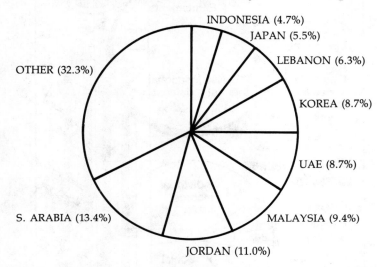

Source: American Language Institute, The University of Toledo.

1. Which country has the fewest students at the Univ. of Toledo? ____
   _____

2. Which country has the most? _____
   _____

3. Write down three suggestions for the Foreign Student Adviser after
   you study this circle graph or pie chart.
   a. _____
   _____
   b. _____
   _____
   c. _____
   _____

Tables

Columns are used for recording statistics in tables. The following are rules for reading tables:

1. Read the title, or caption, carefully. Raise questions.

2. Note the unit of measurement.

3. Read the headings of the columns.

4. Read the footnotes.

5. Determine the reliability of figures by noting the source and date.

Gross National Product* In Ten Countries in 1981	
Country	**GNP (in billions)**
United States	$12,820
Switzerland	17,430
Somalia	280
Malaysia	1,840
Italy	5,960
Syria	1,570
Saudi Arabia	12,600
Jordan	1,620
Kuwait	20,900
China	300

Source: Adapted from John Paxton (Ed.), *Statesman's Yearbook, 122nd Edition,* New York: St. Martins Press, 1985–86.

*This term is used to measure the total value of all the goods and services produced in the country during the year.

•Outlining a Text

In Unit 3 you learned how an outline looks and how to outline before you write. Outlining can also be helpful to you in your reading; that is, *after* a text has been written. Often when you are reading a particularly long or difficult text, it helps to outline the material to see how it is organized. Understanding the organization of a written text aids you in following (and in remembering) the author's argument or ideas.

Read the following part of a chapter from a business textbook. Then study the outline that follows it.

What Is Business?*

The term "business" means different things to different people. To some it means IBM, General Motors, Gulf Oil, and the many other very large organizations we hear of every day. To others, business means a job. Still others think of it as a small family enterprise that's been their livelihood for many years. In its more far-reaching sense, business can be thought of as a social process involving the assembly and utilization of productive resources to produce products and services capable of satisfying society's needs and wants. In this sense, business is as much a part of the social system of the Soviet Union or the People's Republic of China as it is of the United States. Regardless of a nation's political structure, economic goods and services must be produced and distributed. What distinguishes American business firms from Russian or Chinese firms is our almost complete reliance on individual decision making, guided by the profit motive, to determine the output of goods and services. In collectivist economies, central planning replaces private initiative to a very large extent.

All business firms, those run by individuals, as well as those centrally planned, employ six basic resources: people, money, machines, materials, methods, and markets. These six resources are the basic inputs and outputs that are common to all productive activity.

I. **What is business?**

    A. **It is the assembly and utilization of productive resources to produce products and services capable of satisfying society's needs and wants.**

    B. **It is the reliance on individualized decision making: unlike USSR and PRC.**

    C. **It is guided by a profit motive.**

*Lawrence J. Gitman and Carl McDaniel, Jr., *Business World* (New York: John Wiley & Sons, 1983), Chapter 1.

D. It is the employment of these 6 basic resources by business firms.

1. people   4. materials

2. money   5. methods

3. machines   6. markets

Notice in the outline how the countries' names—the Soviet Union and China—have been abbreviated as *USSR* and *PRC* and how the word *six* has been written as a number. As you will see in the following unit on Notemaking, abbreviations can be useful when outlining a text.

For practice in outlining a textbook, go on to *exercise 29*.

Exercise 29: Outlining a Textbook

Read the following passage and outline it in topic form. Then compare your outline with the one on pages 96 and 97.

There are five layers of atmosphere around the earth. There are the *troposphere, stratosphere, mesosphere, exosphere,* and *ionosphere.* The *troposphere* is the lowest layer of atmosphere and is closest to the surface of the earth. It extends to a height of ten to eleven miles in tropical regions and to five to six miles in regions nearer the poles. Four fifths of the atmospheric mass is contained in the troposphere. Temperatures range from −60° to −110° F. The *stratosphere* is above the troposphere. The temperature in the lower part is constant with the height. In the higher part, the temperature increases with the height. At thirty miles, the temperature is 45° F. Jet planes fly in this layer. The *mesosphere* is above the stratosphere and has temperatures of 100° F at fifty miles. This layer burns meteors. Beyond the mesosphere, above 300 miles, is the *exosphere.* Here, the earth's atmosphere merges with gases of interplanetary space. Space in the exosphere appears to be empty. The *ionosphere* covers an area from 50 to 300 miles beyond the earth. It contains electrically charged particles or IONS, as well as neutral molecules, and that is where this layer got its name. Auroral displays occur in this area. The ionosphere is used in radio communications for reflecting signals over long distances.*

*Paraphrased from *Encyclopedia Americana* (1989), pp. 628–31, an article by Robert G. Fleagle.

ATMOSPHERE

I. Troposphere

    A. Closest to the earth

    B. Height

        1. 10 to 11 miles in tropical regions

        2. 5 to 6 miles nearer to poles

    C. Contains 4/5 of atmospheric mass

    D. Temps: $-60°$ to -110 F

    E. Storms occur here

II. Stratosphere

    A. Above the troposphere

    B. Temperatures

        1. Constant with height in the lower part

        2. Increases with height in higher part

        3. At thirty miles, 45°F

    C. Jet planes fly here

III. Mesosphere

    A. Above the stratosphere

    B. Temperature: 100°F at 50 miles

    C. Burns meteors

IV. Exosphere

    A. Beyond the mesosphere: above 300 miles

    B. Earth's atmosphere merges with gases of interplanetary space

    C. Empty space

V. Ionosphere

    A. Beyond exosphere: 50 to 300 miles past earth

B. Electrically charged IONS

C. Auroral displays

D. Reflects radio signals

•Mapping

Apart from outlining, there are other ways to record the organization of a text. One of these ways is *mapping*. Mapping is a method of diagramming the main points of a written or spoken text. As an example, *reread* the text about the atmosphere on p. 95, Exercise 29. Then look at the "map" or diagram of that text below.

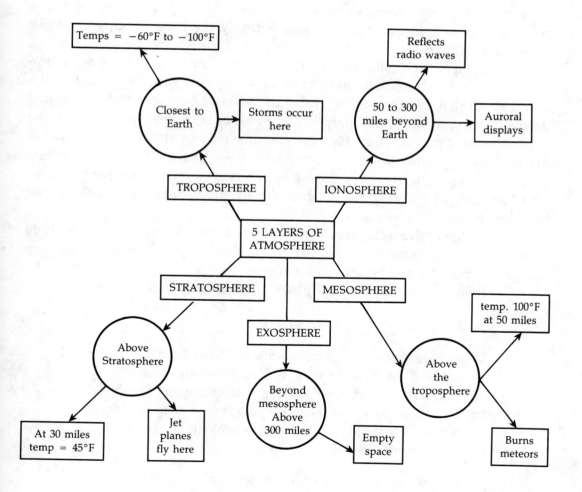

Notice the use of a central rectangle to express the textbook's title. Lines radiating from the center to large circles or balloons indicate the five major points or topics of the reading; smaller rectangles connected to the circles indicate the supporting statements or details of the text. The overall effect or impression is a map.

For some people, the vertical organization of an outline is easier for them to recognize and remember. For others, however, the "map" is a more useful reading aid.

●Summarizing

Previewing, skimming, scanning, outlining, and mapping are ways to help you understand, record, and remember what you read. *Summarizing* is another way to help you recall and retain the information you read. In summarizing, you say or write down only the most important points. Those points may contain a general idea, as well as several details. But only the most important idea or details are included.

For example, think of a movie or a TV show you have recently seen, or a short story or book you may have read. Now imagine you are going to tell a friend about that movie or story. Recall the main idea or plot and any related details. Then, prepare a summary of the movie or story that includes only the most important points. Your summary could be either written or oral, depending on how you wish to communicate with your friend. The purpose of the summary, for you, is to convey the major points, as a review of what you have heard or read; for your friend, the summary is an overview of something that that person has not experienced directly.

Look at the end of a chapter in one of your course textbooks. Does it include a summary? Very often textbook writers include chapter summaries to help students remember and review each chapter.

The following paragraph might be a summary for *Unit 3* of this book:

SUMMARY

If you have read this chapter carefully and have taken the time to do each exercise, you should have a working knowledge of expository writing. You have learned about paragraph structure and the logical development of an idea; you have learned how to use transitional phrases in order to make ideas flow from one sentence to the next; and you have learned the basic structure of an essay.

For practice in summarizing a written text, go on to *exercise 30*.

Exercise 30: Summarizing

Read the text below, noting the main idea and details. Then write a summary of no more than one third the length of the original text. Compare your summary with the one on page 100.

Apes*

Many apes bear a striking resemblance to human beings. They belong to the family of animals called primates.

There are two groups of apes: the great apes and the lesser ape. Among the great apes are included the chimpanzees, gorillas, and orangutans. The lesser ape is called a gibbon.

All of these apes have many things in common. First of all, they have hairy, tailless bodies with longer arms than legs. They have longer fingers than toes, but have only minimal thumbs. In addition, they have a large brain and are supposed to be the most intelligent of the animals. Apes have common ancestors with humans.

Marsha L. Botsford

*Condensed from *World Book Encyclopedia* (1986), pp. 527–28, an article by J.R. Napier.

Most apes live in tropical Africa and Asia. Gorillas, which eat ground plants, are decreasing in number. Apes are often sold to zoos or to research centers. At the present time, cities and farms are replacing the forests where the great apes once lived. Humans need to solve this serious problem before apes become extinct.

Write your summary in the space below.

Summary of Exercise 30 Text

Apes, which resemble human beings, live primarily in Africa and Asia, and belong to the primate family. The number of apes is decreasing. Of the two groups of apes, great apes include chimpanzees, gorillas, and orangutans; the lesser ape is the gibbon. All apes are hairy, with long arms and fingers, a large brain and tailless bodies.

EXTENSION ACTIVITIES

1. Skim the headlines and lead sentences of three paragraphs in your local or daily newspaper. Write down three questions—one for each paragraph—that your skimming made you want to ask.

2. Go to your dictionary and scan the key words (at the top right and left corners of each page) for a page containing the first three letters of your name. Next, scan that page for words that you recognize from your reading. Write down the words and whatever definition comes to mind when you see the word. Then compare your definitions with those in the dictionary.

3. Locate a globe, a map, or an atlas, and look at one country. Describe what you see using whatever information that particular graphic aid provides about location and topography.

4. "Map" Unit 4 of this book, then write a summary of its contents. You can do the same thing for the other units of the book.

Answers to Exercises

pp. 75, 76 **Paragraph 1: b; paragraph 2: c**

p. 77 **1.** 1929.

p. 78 **2.** "the problems of how the peoples of the world could begin to understand each other and get along in peaceful coexistence"

p. 78 **1.** This book is intended for instructors and intermediate-to-advanced–level students in intensive English programs (IEPs) in the United States.
2. It may also be of interest to ESL students in regular university-level English, speech, and communication courses and/or to ESL/EFL students in colleges and private programs abroad.
3. It is designed for use as a textbook-workbook for the whole class and on an individual student basis.

p. 81 **Graph A: 1.** a line graph **2.** "Grades of International Students in One Engineering Class **3.** number of students **4.** the students' grades **5.** that student's grade **6.** student 5 **7.** student 2 **8.** 3.1

p. 83 **Graph B: 1.** the date **2.** one million tons **3.** by solid or broken lines **4.** number of tons in a particular year **5.** 1972/1982 **6.** 4 times

p. 84 **Graph C: 1.** a bar graph **2.** grades of international students in an engineering class **3.** student number **4.** G.P.A. **5.** the grade of a particular student **6.** #5 **7.** #2 **8.** 3.1

p. 85 **Graph D: 1., 2., 3., 4.** draw your own conclusions or assumptions

p. 86 **Graph E: 1., 2, 3,** Think about what the men purchased and compare that with what you know about good nutrition

p. 87 **Graph F: 1.** a circle or pie chart **2.** student body at State University **3.** percentage of students **4.** yes/university records

p. 89 **Graph G: 1.** a line graph **2.** highway deaths (1985 to 1989) **3.** the year **4.** number of deaths in thousands from 0 to 48,000 **5.** number of deaths that year **6.** 1988 **7.** number of deaths in a particular year

p. 90 **Graph H: 1.** circle or pie chart **2.** where fatal accidents occurred **3.** U.S./state highways **4.** National Highway Traffic Safety Administration/yes

p. 91 **Graph I: 1.** circle graphs or pie charts **2.** the Federal Budget **3.** where money is spent; where money comes from **4.** government subsidies **5.** taxes on gasoline, liquor, and tobacco **6.** White House Budget Office/yes

p. 92 **Graph J: 1.** Indonesia **2.** other

Unit 5
Practicing Notemaking

● Notemaking While Reading (Answer Yes or No)

Do you know how to make notes from a written text?   p. 104

● Using Abbreviations

Do you know what abbreviations *are?*   p. 104

Do you know how to use abbreviations when you write?   pp. 105–108

● Notemaking While Listening

Do you know how to make notes from a lecture or a spoken text?   pp. 105–115

If you answered "NO" to any of the questions above, read the indicated pages and do the corresponding exercises.

•Notemaking While Reading

In Units 3 and 4, you learned about outlining and mapping and how to raise and answer questions about what you read. You also learned how to read for the main idea (skimming) and for details (scanning). In doing the exercises, you probably copied down information from the text to answer specific questions or to express your own ideas. You may even have underlined parts of a reading or you may have written notes in the margin of the page to help you recognize and remember important information. If you did write in your book, next to a text that you were reading, you are already performing a kind of task called *notemaking.* Notemaking is a form of outlining that involves identifying and recording, in shortened form, the topic sentences and major supporting sentences of a written text. The "notes" that you make may be copied as sentences in your book (usually in the margin of the page) or expressed in your own words. The purpose of notemaking, as with outlining, is to provide you with a written reminder of the content of a particular paragraph or chapter. The reminder, or note, should be brief and to the point, expressing only the essence of what you have read.

Unlike *notetaking,* or the actual recording word-by-word of what you hear or read, *notemaking* involves synthesizing or pulling together words and ideas to make a note worth remembering.

•Using Abbreviations

Since the function of notemaking is to remind you of certain ideas, entire words are often omitted or written down in a shortened form known as *abbreviations.* The use of abbreviations makes notemaking easier and allows you to record information more rapidly than if you were to write a complete sentence, phrase, or word.

Read the following introduction to a chapter entitled "The American Business System" from a college-level textbook. As you read, notice the main ideas and important details and supports. See if you can identify the "stepladder" organization discussed in Unit 3. Then study the notes that were made from the written text. Notice particularly the use of abbreviations and symbols. Can you identify the words from the abbreviations?

The American Business System*

Introduction

The business system that exists in the United States today is both dynamic and interesting. The variety of ways that people can exchange goods and services (and make money in the process) is amazing. Such innovation is channeled by laws and customs, and by basic business relationships. The latter is our focus in this chapter.

Some believe that business in the United States moved into a new phase in the 1980s. The steady rise in the standard of living in the 1950s and 1960s changed during the decade of the 1970s. People had to scramble to maintain their living standard against rising inflation. The American people seemed to change their ideas about the future. As a result, future consumer buying patterns will probably be less predictable than in the past.

To understand how business is related to our economic system, we could begin with inflation, productivity, the way markets work—all current topics. But we need to have a perspective on our subject before going too deeply into complex issues. Let us consider first some basic relationships between business and economics. Then we can look at how a private enterprise economy like ours operates, the economic goals of the United States, and the factors of production. We then turn to the way markets work and what determines business climate.

Outline of *The American Business System*

Introduction

1. **The bus. sys. in US today = both dynamic & interesting**

2. **Some believe bus. in US moved into new phase in 1980s**

   a. **Rise in standard of living in 50s & 60s—changed in 70s**

      1) **Rising inflation**

      2) **Changed ideas about future**

      a) **future buying patterns—less predictable**

*Vernon A. Musselman and John H. Jackson, *Introduction to Modern Business*, 9th ed. (Englewood Cliffs, NJ: Prentice Hall, 1984), pp. 3–10.

3. Bus. related to econ. sys. w/inflation, productivity, & the way markets work

   a. Rel. bet. bus. & econ.

      1) How pvt. ent. econ. operates, econ. goals, & the factors of production

   b. How markets work & what determines bus. climate

Now, without looking back at the text, see how many of the following abbreviations you can identify. Write the full words next to the abbreviations and symbols.

bus. sys. _____

US _____

= _____

& _____

Rel. bet. bus. & econ. _____

pvt. ent. _____

w/ _____

You can find many common and widely accepted abbreviations in a good standard dictionary. Check the Contents page of your dictionary and see if it contains separate sections on abbreviations and special symbols. If it doesn't, you might want to purchase a dictionary that does, or at least familiarize yourself with the information about abbreviations so that it can assist you in your notemaking.

Everyone has his or her own system of making notes, however. If you already have a way of abbreviating words and writing symbols, you are on your way to being a notemaker!

For more practice in recognizing and using abbreviations and symbols, turn to *p. 107, exercise 31.*

Exercise 31: Using Abbreviations in Notemaking

Try to identify the following abbreviations and symbols. Then read the passage below and make notes in the right margin of this exercise sheet, using abbreviations. Compare your notes with those in the rough outline.

1.   &   4. ltd.

2. deals w/   5. prob.

3. thru   6. prods.

We are all involved in business. In the United States, the basic necessities, such as food, shelter, and clothing, are delivered by our business system. Underlying this system is a basic mechanism that determines how products and services of all kinds will be delivered. It is called *economics*.

Economics affects all of us, whether we understand it or not. Economics is a science that deals with the satisfaction of human wants through scarce resources. Since all resources are limited, there are never enough to give people all they want. The economic system of a country must deal with the problem of allocating these scarce resources among the competing parties who want them, and deciding among the variety of products that might be produced.*

A rough outline from reading passage in Exercise 31

I. **Bus. & econ.**
   Intro.

   1. **All involved in bus.**

      a. **Basic needs: food, shelter & clothing = delivered by bus. sys.**

         1. **Basic sys. = economics**

         2. **Econ. = a science that deals w/ the satisfaction of human wants thru scarce resources**

*Vernon A. Musselman and John H. Jackson, *Introduction to Modern Business*, 9th ed. (Englewood Cliffs, NJ: Prentice Hall, 1984), pp. 3–10.

a) Problem: allocating those resources

2. Deciding which prods are produced

For further practice in notemaking, open one of your course textbooks and start reading! If you feel uncomfortable about writing in your own book, make notes on a separate piece of paper. Of course you should never write in any book that is not your own, such as one borrowed from the library, a classmate, or a friend.

Laima Druskis

•Notemaking While Listening

In the same way that you make notes from a textbook, you can make notes from a lecture. The difference, of course, is that unless the person speaking has provided you with a paper or an outline of his or her remarks, you will probably need to supply your own paper or notebook in which to record your notes.

Notemaking from lectures is especially important in large colleges and universities. Classes may be crowded and there may be less opportunity for direct student-teacher interaction. In addition, since lectures are generally not written down and distributed, students must rely on what they hear and on their lecture notes to remind them of a lecture's content.

How can you make good notes from a lecture? First of all, you need to listen carefully for **key words** and **phrases** that tell you what ideas the speaker feels are important. Words such as *first (of all)*, *secondly*, *thirdly*, *next*, *then* and *finally* indicate the order in which things occur or are organized. Other phrases such as *in summary*, *in conclusion*, and *to sum up* tell you that the speaker's remarks are coming to an end. Many of the words and phrases good speakers use in oral presentations can be found among the transitions listed in Unit 3: Organizing Your Writing. Review those words and listen for them in the lectures you hear; they will help you follow the organization of the speaker's comments.

You can also observe the way the speaker uses his or her voice and body to emphasize parts of a lecture. While you cannot make notes on the way a person stands or speaks, you can perhaps get a better idea of what the speaker is trying to say by noticing how the hands are used and how the voice increases or decreases in volume. Notice also how questions are used to focus attention on a certain point.

Now listen as your instructor reads a lecture to you on why we should study biology as a science. As you listen, try to determine the lecture's organization. Can you identify the "steps" of generality? (See unit 3.) Make notes of the lecture on a separate piece of paper. Write on only one side of your paper and leave wide margins. In that way you can later add any information or details you may have missed. Use whatever abbreviations you find helpful. Then compare your notes with those outlined on p. 110. (The steps of generality have been inserted in the text of the lecture, below.)

Text of a lecture on biology.

Why Should We Study Biology as a Science? *

1. Why should we study science and, in particular, why should we study biology? *2.* First of all, let us focus on the first part of the question: science. *3.* One excellent reason is to understand the world we live in. *4.* Scientific knowledge of our physical surroundings is useful to all of us. *3.* Another reason might be to prepare for a career in science. *4.* Many people enjoy science so much, however, that they

*Adapted from James M. Barrett, Peter Abramoff, A. Krishna Kumaran, and William S. Millington, *Biology* (Englewood Cliffs, NJ: Prentice Hall, 1986), p. 1.

study it mostly for the personal satisfaction that mastery of a demanding and interesting subject provides. *3.* However, there are good reasons why educated people should have a firm grasp of fundamental scientific principles and methods. *4.* By its continuing demand for exactness and objectivity, laboratory research is one of the best disciplinarians when it comes to developing habits of patience and reserve in forming judgments until all pertinent evidence is considered. *4.* Although the study of science is not unique in its ability to provide the benefits derived from scholarly endeavor, it is an important and exciting field of inquiry, as beneficial as any other in this regard.

2. Second, why should we study biology? *3.* The study of biology, like that of any other natural science, provides all the benefits noted above, but it does more. *4.* It provides insights into the living world of which we humans are an integral part. *4.* We thus come to understand ourselves better through such a course of study, and being knowledgeable about a subject of growing social importance worldwide, we are able to become better citizens as well. *4.* When you plan your course of study in a university, it would be wise to consider these benefits.

Notes from lecture:

Why study science/biol.?

I. Science

    A. to understand world we live in

        1. scientif. know. of phys. world is useful

    B. to prep. for a career

        1. for personal satis.

    C. educated pple: grasp of scientif. princips.

        1. lab. res. = good disciplinar.

        2. an imp. exciting field of inq.

II. Biol.

    A. provides benefits of science *plus*

        1. insights into living world of hums.

2. we understand selves; better citizens

3. conclusion

The above notes contain a lot of abbreviations. See how many of them you can identify *before* you go back to the reading text to check your answers. Compare your notes with the ones above. Are your notes indented to indicate ideas of greater and lesser importance? Did you use numbers and letters to show how the lecture was organized? Which of the abbreviations in the outlined notes did you use also? Which words did you write out in full?

Remember, abbreviations are a way to help you save time in your notemaking. But your abbreviations should be clear and remind you of specific words or concepts. If an abbreviation is unclear to you and does not bring an immediate idea or word to mind, then it probably is not the best abbreviation for you to use.

For additional practice in notemaking while listening, turn to *p. 112, exercise 32.*

Exercise 32: Notemaking While Listening

Listen as your instructor reads a lecture to you entitled "Going to College or University in the United States." Using whatever abbreviations you like, make notes below or on a separate sheet of paper on the topic sentences and supporting statements of the lecture. Then arrange your notes in outline form and compare your outline with the one on page 113. (Notice the use of abbreviations.)

Text of lecture for Exercise 32, (Steps of generality have been marked.):

Going to College or University in the United States

Selecting the right school is a very important decision to make. Things to be considered are the *entrance requirements, costs, accreditation, curriculum* suited to your major interests, *a good intensive English program,* and the *size* of the university.

1. There are several things you should *consider* if you are planning to attend a university in the U.S. *2.* First, there are many *kinds of colleges and universities. 3.* There are *private* schools that are financed by *endowments;* there are *church* controlled schools, usually dominated by *one religion;* and there are *public* schools financed by *state tax dollars.*

2. Second, *campus organizations* can meet some of your educational and social needs. *3.* Many universities have *international student organizations, campus clubs, student organizations,* and *fraternities and sororities.*

2. Third, the *curriculum* should be an important consideration for you. Universities have *various colleges* that offer many different courses. *3.* There are *liberal arts* colleges and *courses, scientific and technological schools* and *courses, undergraduate and graduate courses,* professional courses, and so on. *3.* There are also a number of *different degrees,* such as the undergraduate *B.A.* (bachelor of arts) and *B.S.* (bachelor of science), the graduate *M.A.* (master of arts) and *M.S.* (master of science), or the *M.B.A.* (masters in business administration) and *M.A.T.* (master of arts in teaching), and the highest degree, the *Ph.D.* (doctor of philosophy) or *Ed.D.* (doctor of education).

2. Finally, you should explore *living arrangements* and *community services* and facilities before you go to a university in the United States. *3.* Find out about the availability of housing in *dormitories* or nearby *apartments;* look into the proximity of *shops, health facilities,* and the *library;* inquire about *research opportunities* and/or opportunities for academic help through *tutors;* and be sure to ask what *sports activities, exercise programs,* and *social events* you can participate in. As you can see, there is much to consider when selecting the right school.

Notes for lecture in Exercise 32:

Going to Coll. or Univ. in the U.S.

I. Selecting the right school

A. Entrance requires.

B. Costs

C. Accreditation

D. Curriculum

E. A good I.E.P.

F. Size

II. Considerations

A. Kinds of colls. & univs.

1. private: endowments

2. church: one religion

3. public: state tax $

B. Campus orgs.

1. internatl. student orgs.

2. campus clubs

3. student orgs.

4. fraterns. & sorors.

C. Curriculum

1. various colls.

a. lib. arts. courses

b. sci. & tech. courses

c. undergrad. & grad. courses

2. diff. degrees

a. B.A. and B.S.

b. M.A. and M.S.

c. M.B.A. and M.A.T.

d. Ph.D. and Ed.D.

D. **Living arrangements & commun. servs.**

    1. **dorms or apts.**

    2. **shops, health facils., lib.**

    3. **research opps., tutors**

    4. **sports activs., exercise progs., social events**

It is always a good idea to review your lecture notes with another student in the same class as soon after a lecture as possible. By reviewing while the material is still fresh in your mind, you can correct any errors in your notes before you arrange them in final outline form.

In your next lecture class, try implementing some of the notemaking tips you learned in this unit. You might want to tape record a lecture or two in the beginning to help you get started. Pay attention to the transition words and phrases the speaker uses, and practice making notes from your tape. As your notemaking skills improve, you will find yourself becoming less dependent on your cassette recorder and more dependent on your ears, eyes, and hand to make good, efficient notes.

EXTENSION ACTIVITIES

1. Turn to the first part of Unit 5 and make notes on p. 104 (up to the reading entitled "The American Business System"). Use abbreviations.

2. Turn on the radio or TV in time for the morning or evening news. Make notes on what you hear, using abbreviations. Afterwards, arrange your notes in outline form.

3. Make notes of the lecture portion of the class in which you are using this book. Use abbreviations. After class, review your notes with a friend and see if you agree on what material your instructor covered.

Answers to Exercises
Exercise 31:   *1.* and   *2.* deals with   *3.* through   *4.* limited   *5.* problem   *6.* products

Unit 6
Taking Exams

●Preparing for an Exam (Answer Yes or No)

Do you use good study habits when you are preparing for an exam?

p. 118

●Knowing about Different Exams

Are you familiar with the different kinds of school examinations?

pp. 119–124

●Taking an Exam

Do you do these things when you take an exam: *pp. 120–122*

- read the directions carefully?
- pace yourself?
- review?
- mark your answer clearly?
- guess?

If you answered "NO" to any of the above questions, read the indicated pages and do the corresponding exercises.

•Preparing for Exams

Examinations, or "exams" as they are popularly called, are the way people connected with schools or other aspects of your life evaluate your performance. Exams are also a way of informing you of your current progress and ability.

There are many factors that influence exam or test performance, some having little to do with your knowledge of a subject. However, it can be said that people who prepare for exams generally have a better chance of performing well on them than those people who do not prepare.

How do *you* prepare for an exam? Which of the following phrases best describes you and your study habits?

A	**B**
• Study a little every day.	• Postpone studying until exam time.
• Exercise regularly.	• Exercise irregularly.
• Eat well.	• Eat when there's time.
• Review the night before the exam.	• Study everything for the first time the night before the exam.
• Go to bed before midnight.	• Stay up all night studying.
• Get up early for a last review.	• Sleep in late.
• Arrive at the exam site in time to get a good seat.	• Arrive at the exam site just in time to be admitted.
• Bring a good supply of pens and sharpened pencils with erasers.	• Forget to bring pens and pencils.

If you checked any of the descriptions in Column B, you need to examine your own behavior and study habits as they relate to your exam and academic performance. You may need to review some of Unit 1 and the discussion of good study habits. Unless you have established good study habits, it will be difficult for you to perform well in school.

•Knowing about Different Exams

Good study habits and knowledge of your subject area are a good start. But knowing something about the different kinds of exams can also be of help.

In general there are two basic exam types: objective exams and subjective exams. The former type usually includes true/false, multiple choice, fill-in-the-blank, and matching tests; the latter typically includes written essays and oral presentations.

Objective Exams

Most of the standardized tests given students these days are objective, such as the SAT, LSAT, GRE, GMAT, and the TOEFL. Many classroom tests given by individual instructors may also be of the objective type. Some standardized tests—the international TOEFL, for example—may also include a subjective part (a 30-minute essay) in addition to the objective test questions.

The following is a brief description of the kinds of objective tests just mentioned.

True/False: Statements are given for which students must mark *True* (or *T*) if the statement is true of *False* (or *F*) if the statement is false.

Multiple choice: Students must choose one of several choices (usually 4 and usually indicated by letters *a, b, c,* or *d*).

Matching: Students match words, phrases, formulas, numbers and so on, from one list with those on a second list, usually opposite the first list on the same page.

Fill-in-the-blank: Students complete a sentence with a missing word or words either from a list, words in parentheses, or from memory.

Subjective Exams

Unlike objective tests requiring a minimal response, subjective exams, such as essay exams and oral presentations, require you, the "subject," to present your ideas and opinions in a logical manner, based on your knowledge of the subject area or field. Subjective exams tend to give you more freedom than objective exams, in which exact answers are expected. However, increased freedom also means increased responsibility to make sure that your ideas are organized and presented in an orderly and appropriate fashion.

•Taking an Exam

In any exam, objective or subjective, there are directions or instructions to the student explaining what has to be done. These directions are frequently followed by an example. When taking an exam, the first thing to do once the exam has begun is to read the directions carefully. By reading the directions, you will learn what the examiners' expectations are and what, if any, policy there is regarding guessing. In objective exams especially, such as the GRE, for example, there may be a penalty, or loss of points, for an incorrect answer. On such exams, then, it would be better not to guess unless you were fairly certain that your answer was correct. However, other tests, such as the TOEFL, encourage guessing by considering incorrect any unmarked answers. So, on the TOEFL, it is to your advantage to guess when you aren't sure of an answer.

After reading the general exam directions, be sure to notice the time limit, if any, and check your watch or a clock in the exam room so that you will know what time the exam will end. Keep track of the time as you progress through the exam so that you are not surprised when the examiner announces the end of the exam.

Once you have read the directions and noted the time, you are ready to begin answering the test questions. As you proceed through the exam, be sure to read each question thoroughly. If any question requires some thought or extra time, skip it and go on to other test items that you know. You can always put a *light* pencil mark next to the number of the item you are skipping. That way you will be able to return to the item later on during the exam. If, after you complete the exam, you have some remaining time, reread the exam and recheck your answers. Do not change any answers unless you are quite sure that the change will make the answer correct.

Taking Objective Exams

Below are some specific hints and suggestions regarding specific objective exams.

True/False: Beware of words such as *always, only, never,* and *none.* Such words usually predict a False answer. On the other hand, words such as *sometimes* and *usually* often lead to the answer True. Read each test question carefully, however, and use these clues advisedly. The sentences *The sun always rises in the east* and *None of the members of that remote New Guinea tribe have ever been to America* are True, of course, despite the use of the words *always* and *none*.

Some instructors, when creating true/false tests, often include more true than false statements because they want to reinforce, with accurate statements, what you have learned. On an objective test where there is no penalty for guessing, then, it would be wise to guess *true* for every unanswered test item.

Multiple Choice: In these exams you can often arrive at the correct answer by the process of elimination. For example, if the question asks, *How many days are there in a year?* and gives the following choices: *a) 42, b) 365, c) 1150, and d) 220,* you could probably eliminate choices a), c), and d) right away. Whether or not you knew the correct answer is *365,* doesn't matter; you arrived at it just the same, by taking away the answers that were obviously incorrect.

Matching: These exams generally ask you to compare items in two columns facing each other on a page. By crossing off each item as you "match" it with another item, you can keep track of which answers you have used and which ones are still available to be used. You also avoid using the same answer more than once.

Fill-ins: In these exams there is also a danger of repeating one or more possible answers. Be sure to cross off answers as you use them. Again, be careful to read the instructions to make certain that you are filling in the blanks in the requested way.

Taking Subjective Exams

When you take an essay exam, the directions are particularly important and can mean the difference between passing or failing the exam. Test makers are accustomed to using certain key or clue words to indicate what you are supposed to do. For example, if a question asks you to "compare and contrast kinetic energy with geothermal energy," be sure that you give *both* similarities and differences.

There are many other clue words that appear on essay exams. Study the list below and be sure you are familiar with each of the words mentioned:

compare – examine the characteristics in order to determine the similarities

contrast – examine the characteristics in order to discover the differences

define – give clear and concise definitions

describe – relate exactly what happened or what something is like, using descriptive writing

diagram – illustrate the answer with an accurately labeled graphic aid

discuss – analyze all sides of the question in detail, using expository writing

explain – answer the why? how? where? and who? and give relevant differences of opinion

illustrate – draw a graphic aid or else give a clear, concise example

justify – give proof or cite evidence to support an idea

outline – organize your answer, then make an outline of the facts or information you have

review – analyze the material by giving an organized presentation of the main ideas

summarize – connect all of the major supports or facts, using transitional words or phrases

As with objective tests, be sure to read all of the directions first and make certain you understand what you are to do. In essay exams, pay attention to the verbs *compare, contrast, discuss, explain,* and so on. Read the *entire exam* through, before you start to write or answer.

Also note how much time each question is allotted and plan the use of your time. Use three or four minutes to make an outline of your answer to each question. Answer *first* the question that carries the most points on the exam. *(Do not forget to number your answer!)* Make sure you include a thesis statement in the introduction of your essay answer, topic sentences for your supporting paragraphs or the body of your essay, and an appropriate conclusion. And tie everything together by including transitional words and phrases. Then review your grammar and spelling before you turn in your paper.

Patrick Watson

Making Oral Presentations

Like essay exams, oral exams or presentations require you to "present" your knowledge of a subject. Your presentation, however, is to a listening, rather than to a reading, audience. And just as your essay will be judged on content and form or structure, your oral presentation will be evaluated in terms of content and delivery. When preparing your presentation, keep these things in mind: time allotted for speaking (Should you leave time at the end for questions?); number of topics to be covered; audio or visual aids to be used; and handouts for the audience.

When making your presentation, be sure to:

Face your audience and look directly at different people from time to time

Glance down at your notes (use 3" × 5" index cards) but *do not read them*

Speak in a clear voice at natural speed and volume.

Try not to hurry or to speak too slowly; check your audience occasionally to be sure people are following ("Am I speaking too fast/slowly?" "Are you following me?"). **If you do use audio-visual equipment, be sure to test it** *in advance* **so that you know it is in working order.** Also be sure to introduce your audio or visual illustrations at the appropriate points and cite any research necessary to support your remarks.

As with an essay, an oral presentation should include an introduction, supporting paragraphs, transitions, and a conclusion. And, if it is well planned, your presentation should be a performance that you, as well as your audience, enjoys.

EXTENSION ACTIVITIES

1. Prepare a short (5–10 minutes) speech about your country. Include three things you think others should or would like to know about it. Practice your speech in front of a friend or in front of the mirror. Pay attention to your body language and eye contact. Then, give your speech to a small group or members of your class. Ask for feedback (comments) on your presentation.

2. Write an essay in which you compare and contrast the education system of your country to that of the United States. Consult your library for any information you need before you write. Be sure to cover both countries in your paper.

3. If you are unfamiliar with the different standardized tests offered in the United States and required for university admission, consult the librarian at your school and/or check a local bookstore for copies of any available test preparation booklets, such as the TOEFL, GRE, or LSAT prep books.

Summary

If you have read and studied this book carefully, you should have acquired study habits that facilitate both language learning and subject-area learning. You should also have acquired language skills that can be transformed into study skills. To do this took planning, effort, and concentration, and you are to be commended for your hard work.

But working hard is what being a scholar is all about! If you do not work hard and apply yourself to the task, you will not experience the great satisfaction of learning something new.

As long as you have invested the time, expense, and energy to attend an American university, you should do your best to become an educated person. And you can do this by getting involved in the search for knowledge by listening to others, reading widely, and, finally, by reaching your own version of the truth.

Glossary of Key Words

The following key words and phrases appear, in the order indicated, in Units 1–6 of *Language and Study Skills for Learners of English.* Make sure you are familiar with these words and expressions.

Unit 1
student services
administrative offices
dormitories
financial aid
scholarships
student loans
health insurance
student I.D.
counseling
advisor
study habits
English-only dictionary
facilitate
Ph.D. and Ed.D.
status
outlines
summary
plagiarism
librarian
inventory
library holdings
open stacks
atlases
notation
annually
circulate
check out
current events

Unit 2
word collector
index cards
part of speech
definition
alphabetical order
bilingual
monolingual
inflections
etymology
hyphenated
synonyms
antonyms
slang
colloquial expressions
abbreviations
pronunciation
syllables
affixes
prefix
suffix
stem

Unit 3
topic outline
sentence outline
general to specific
ladders of generality
topic heads

Roman numerals
arabic numbers
indentation
alignment
parallelism
transitions
autobiography
paragraph
topic sentence
supporting sentences
concluding sentence
summarize
controlling (or main) idea
detail
coherent
expository writing
descriptive writing
narrative writing
essay
thesis statement
topic controls
indent
brainstorm

Unit 4
preview
sections
formulate questions
predict answers
preface
overview
chapter
chapter headings
graphic aids
skimming
scanning
PQ5R
reflect
tables

charts
caption
line graph
bar graph
circle or pie graph
pictograph
horizontal
vertical
percentage
statistics
interpret
segment
atmosphere
mapping
headline

Unit 5
notemaking
notetaking
abbreviations
symbols
lecture
key words
notes
margins
implement

Unit 6
examinations
objective
subjective
GRE
LSAT
TOEFL
clue words
compare
contrast
audio-visual aids
feedback
standardized tests